JED

Fight..
Good Fight..!

Grace + Peace!

Eloy
John 330!

DON'T GIVE UP

KEYS TO PERSEVERE

ELOY PUGA

LifeRich
PUBLISHING

LifeRich Publishing is a registered trademark of
The Reader's Digest Association, Inc.

LifeRich Publishing books may be ordered
through booksellers or by contacting:

LifeRich Publishing
1663 Liberty Drive
Bloomington, IN 47403
www.liferichpublishing.com
844-686-9607

ISBN: 978-1-4897-3591-1 (sc)
ISBN: 978-1-4897-3592-8 (e)

Print information available on the last page.

LifeRich Publishing rev. date: 05/17/2021

Dedicated to all God seekers
who are awaiting the Lord Jesus' return.
He's coming for us as He said He would.
John 14.1-3

CONTENTS

Introduction...ix

1   No Matter What, Don't Give Up..........................1
2   Pain, Don't Give Up 17
3   Pressure, Don't Give Up....................................39
4   Perplexed, Don't Give Up 59
5   Persecution, Don't Give Up 73
6   Hardships, Don't Give Up..................................99
7   A Time To Give Up...109

I   A Watchman's Unscientific Meditation Of
     Reasonable Random Thoughts.........................117
II   A Message Of True Hope: The Gospel Of
     Jesus Christ 127
III Helpful Resources...131

INTRODUCTION

This message is for the Church of Jesus Christ. It's based on the time-tested truth of God's word, the Bible. Don't give up don't lose heart.

This word of encouragement was placed on my heart while reading 2 Corinthians, the apostle Paul's most personal letter concerning his apostolic calling. Paul, knowing that he was commissioned by God to share God's grace through the Gospel of Jesus Christ, recorded some of the hardships that he and others overcame to fulfill their life's mission. In verses 1 and 16 of chapter four, Paul wrote, "we do not give up." The root of the Greek word translated "give up" is *ekkakeo*. It carries the idea of not to fail, lose courage, faint, or grow weary. It's translated "not lose heart" in Luke 18.1 and "do not grow weary" in Ephesians 3.13 and 2 Thessalonians 3.13 (NIV). The main idea is *don't give up, keep going, keep fighting, keep working, keep pressing on.*

Now is not the time to give up. Too much is at stake. You, me, and somebody in this world need the encouragement to keep pressing on, life changing encouragement to keep going. Within our spheres of influence, we can build people up and inspire them to continue no matter what. After we ourselves are encouraged with truth, the kind of truth that moves so deeply in us that it stimulates us to make the mental and heart resolution to not give up, then we can influence others to do the same. May this word powerfully speak to our hearts and change many lives – it's for God's glory and for our good.

Note: This work is not meant to be an exhaustive study of biblical perseverance. This offering is mainly to encourage the Church to keep the faith in these challenging times as our times continue to get worse. As many things in life overlap, a few chapter themes and keys to victory also overlap. This is beneficial as we learn best through repetition.

Lastly, in this work I write mostly from a first-person plural voice, meaning that I'm writing to you (the reader) while including myself, because I also need to be reminded of these truths and principles. I fully recognize that I'm your fellow sojourner as I write using the word "we." May we be strengthened and encouraged in the Lord!

He's coming soon!

Eloy
John330

NO MATTER WHAT,
DON'T GIVE UP

Facing the reality of ultra-foes of Axis Powers (Nazi Germany, Japan, and Italy) during World War II, UK Prime Minister Winston Churchill urged his audience to never give in no matter what the circumstances were, to never give in to seemingly overwhelming forces, and to be sure that perseverance will lead to victory.[1] Within a few years of those heart-stirring courageous words the Axis Powers were defeated, the world forever changed, and victory was achieved.

Everybody experiences times of feeling like they want to give up, call it quits, and throw in the towel. Life is hard. This is brute fact. No matter what socio-economic environment we were born in, from the ghettos of Detroit, Chicago, or Los Angeles, to the posh suburbs all across the U.S. that have million-dollar

---

[1] Paraphrased from Winston Churchill, "Never Give In, Never, Never, Never" (1941). https://www.nationalchurchillmuseum.org/never-give-in-never-never-never.html.

homes. No matter what our pedigree, from being born to immigrant parents who struggle speaking English to fourth generation citizens of wealthy entrepreneurs, we are people that are frequently faced with adversity and all kinds of challenges.

Yet, without these challenges we would never grow in character, never grow in wisdom, and never grow in understanding. So, life's difficulties could be seen as being invaluable to one's personal development.

Some situations are more difficult than others, and certain situations last longer than others. There may be long seasons of testing that we encounter. Seasons of pain, pressure, confusion, and hardships in which we feel like we just can't keep going. Where we involve both our emotions and our mind as we feel and think: What's the use in continuing? What's the point in this mess? Will this gray cloud that I've been under for days, weeks, years, ever be lifted? Will things ever change? Does God see me? Does He hear me? Does He care about me? Where in the world is He?

I'm here to tell you don't give up. God sees you, hears you, cares for you, and is with you. God honors people of faith who trust Him no matter what. The only true God, the God of Scripture, is faithful to His word and therefore He is faithful to His people. He can be completely trusted, and He has all things under control. There are no maverick molecules in the universe, everything is under the administration of an all-wise, all-powerful, all-caring God that has our best interest at heart.

No matter if our spouse is ready to leave us or if we've been praying for years to find a godly mate, no matter if we just got laid off from our job or we're stressed out at work, no matter if we've been responsible but the bills keep piling up, no matter if it's our third time trying to get off drugs, cigarettes, or alcohol, no matter if we don't know what to do with stressful relationships, no matter if we're sick, no matter if we keep trying to succeed but it seems like all we do is fail, no matter X, no matter Y, and no matter Z. Don't give up. In the end it'll be worth it. Victory is near.

Perseverance, Endurance, and a Reason

Perseverance and Endurance

Before we experience victory, we must add two words to our vocabulary, one is a verb and the other a noun, both are dynamic and work in unison. The first is the verb *persevere* which means *to continue doing something in spite of difficulty or lack of success.* Synonyms include: persist, continue, keep on, keep going, don't take no for an answer, stick to your guns, etc. The perfect antonym to persevere is *give up.*

The other word is the noun *endurance* which is *the ability to do or cope with something painful or difficult for a long time.* Endurance is the quality of lasting a long time before wearing out. Synonyms are: durability, longevity, strength, toughness, and fortitude. The perfect antonym to endurance is weakness. Persevere can be used in the noun form of *perseverance* and is used interchangeably with endurance which shows how closely they're related.

3

One key to effectively not giving up no matter what is to persevere *with* endurance. However, if we think that all we have to do is simply work hard and stir up our human will to push through a situation or reach a goal, we're sadly mistaken. Even though human will is a profoundly remarkable thing that can accomplish much, it will sooner than later expose its insufficiencies. Nevertheless, if we go to God, pray and ask Him to grant us strength to persevere and to bless us with His grace of endurance, this will be a winning combination on our journey toward victory!

The Bible teaches that we can be co-laborers with God in fulfilling His purposes,[2] we're not out here alone striving and dealing with life by ourselves in a strict material realm. No, no, no, a thousand times no! God is always with us and we need a touch of heaven to help us not give up because now is the time to persevere. Let us acknowledge that we must persevere to conquer, we are more than conquerors,[3] and God has much that He purposes to accomplish through us.

No matter if the challenge seems bigger than life, no matter if all looks lost, no matter if we can't see the light at the end of the tunnel, no matter if our emotions can't take it anymore, no matter if our heart can't take it anymore, look to God for the strength to persevere and for His glorious grace of endurance to be abundantly given.

---

[2] 1 Corinthians 3.9.
[3] Romans 8.37.

A Reason

Without an objective, purpose, or a reason to not give up it will be difficult to persevere daily. Yes, life has many purposes throughout, but if we could pinpoint an ultimate purpose and reason for waking up, living, and pressing on, then this makes persevering much sweeter. The Westminster Catechism summarizes the main purpose and reason people should be living for, "What is man's chief end/primary purpose?" Answer, "Man's primary purpose is to glorify God and to enjoy Him forever." We are told that whatever we do we should do it for God's glory.[4] Living for God's honor because of who He is helps us endure our battle through this fallen world.

A change of one's focus to honoring God in all and living under this umbrella gives ultimate direction and meaning to one's life. It doesn't matter which stage of life we're in: childhood, adolescent, young adult, middle age, or senior citizen. It also doesn't matter what we're working toward: a degree, better health, building project, writing a book, raising kids, working on relationships, enhancing or learning a new skill, installing water wells in developing countries, participating athletically for charity, fill in the _____. All should be done to the glory of God. Having a reason that's not in/for our own self-interest helps immensely with drive, motivation, determination, and the execution of persevering.

---

[4] 1 Corinthians 10.31 "Therefore, whether you eat or drink, or whatever you do, do everything for God's glory." In Isaiah 43.7 God says that people were created for His glory ". . . created for My glory."

As people created in the image of God, we're the most important creatures in His eyes. So important are we that God sent His one and only Son, Jesus, to atone for our sins by being a substitute on behalf of all who would ever believe in Him so that the believing sinner would not have to face the wrath of Holy God. There is no greater love than this. This shows that God unconditionally loves people and His purposes are directed toward people. By loving God and loving people, we obey the primary commandments.[5] Perseverance based on glorifying God, loving Him, and loving people helps direct our life's steps while showing in the words of Max Lucado that *It's Not about Me.*[6]

About fifty years before Israel became and was recognized as its own state on May 14, 1948, Theodore Herzl (1860-1904), a Jewish journalist from Vienna, decided to think about God and His people. Herzl saw how Jewish people were being treated in Europe, he quickly recognized where history was headed so he organized and put into motion a vision that developed into the reestablishment of the modern state of Israel.[7]

Herzl, in the midst of opposition, persevered toward

---

[5] Matthew 22.34-39.

[6] Ephesians 2.10 says, "For we are His creation, created in Christ Jesus for good works, which God prepared ahead of time so that we should walk in them." God created us to glorify Him by doing good works toward people on His behalf, not to be self-centered; this honors and pleases God. For the Christian this is not philanthropy, but biblical Christianity.

[7] Thomas Ice, "What Should We Think About the Zionist Movement?," in *What Should We Think About Israel?*, ed. J. Randall Price (Oregon: Harvest House, 2019), 38.

establishing a Jewish homeland because he had his people on his heart. He and like-minded others were instrumental in fulfilling some of God's words that the Jews would be regathered to the land of Israel.[8] "After 2000 years of surviving among nations often hostile to their presence, the Jewish people could return home."[9] Because Theodore Herzl loved and placed others' interests before his own, he played a part in the modern-day miracle re-birth of the Jewish state. Herzl's reason to persevere was both self-less and bigger than him.

The reason Jesus endured hatred, being misunderstood, ridicule, accusations of working for Satan, threats, plots, assaults, a circus trial, beatings, and being nailed to a cross by nine-inch-nails was because He is the King of persevering for others. He laid down His life for others; the Shepherd for the sheep. By taking our place on the cross He was making the way, the only way for us to get to God, the only way for us to be reconciled, the only way for us to be redeemed, the only way for us to be transferred from the kingdom of darkness into God's glorious kingdom, and the only way for humanity to have hope and a future. He went to the cross out of His

---

[8] We can see God's faithfulness to His word and His promises to regather the Jewish people back to the land of Israel in many Scriptures: Isaiah 11.10-12; Jeremiah 29.14; Ezekiel 36.24, 37.21, etc. The ultimate fulfillment of these prophecies will be during the millennium when Jesus reigns as King from Jerusalem – Isaiah 9.6-7; Ezekiel 37.21-28; 2 Samuel 7.12-16, etc.

[9] Elwood McQuaid, *It Is No Dream: Israel: Prophecy and History – The Whole Story* (Bellmawr: Friends of Israel, 2019), Introduction.

gracious love for us, He endured the cross for the joy set before Him.[10]

What should we do? We should follow in His steps. Let's never forget that a call to be a Christian is a call to follow Jesus. Jesus didn't mince words when He said, "If anyone wants to come with me, he must deny himself, take up his cross, and follow Me."[11] Following Jesus is a call to death, a call of dying daily. It's putting God and His purposes primary in our life, a death to self-interest. D. A. Carson clarifies:

> Most of us are not going to be crucified in a literal sense, but we follow a Master who was crucified literally. It is as if Jesus now says, "If I have been crucified, don't you understand? If you are to be my disciple, you must be crucified too" – not, for most of us, in the same physical way he suffered, but in death to self-interest. We are to take up our cross *and follow him*, coming under his lordship as he himself obeyed his own heavenly Father perfectly.[12] (Emphasis in original).

In Jesus' parable of the minas in Luke 19, the King James version reads "Occupy till I come" in verse 13. "Occupy till I come" means that Jesus' followers should be

[10] Hebrews 12.2.

[11] Matthew 16.24. See also the cost of discipleship in Luke 14.25–33.

[12] D. A. Carson, *The God Who Is There: Finding Your Place in God's Story* (Grand Rapids: Baker, 2010), 198.

engaged in His purposes until He returns. The main point of the parable is for Jesus' followers to use what God has given us (skills, talents, gifts, finances, etc.) while awaiting His return, and in return we will ultimately receive His loving approval.[13] Our lives should be primarily focused on God's business of us being His witnesses, His hands, His mouth piece according to His word, evangelizing, discipling, edifying the Church, being salt and light in the world, and so on.

What a great incentive there is in living a life that God approves of. Imagine God, the Creator of all galaxies, announcing His pleasing approval of your life by saying, "well done, good and faithful servant." What a refreshing thought! By being strapped with a reason to live that's bigger than us, not of self-interest and unto God's glory, while focusing on people, persevering through life will still be a challenge, but it'll have immense eternal value.

The Apostle Paul

Nothing of true value ever comes easy. There's a sense of life satisfaction when a tough situation comes to an end after a long fight or when a goal is reached through hard work, determination, and perseverance. Once that life situation turns for the better because of one's refusal to surrender or that goal is finally reached, what was learned through that process can never be taken away, in one sense it becomes part of you. Saul of Tarsus, known as the apostle Paul, is one who knew life's satisfaction in not

---

[13] This parable is similar to the parable of the talents in Matthew 25.14-30.

giving up. He is the most famous missionary in Christian history who experienced victory through excruciating hardships.

In Paul's own words:

> Five times I received 39 lashes from Jews. Three times I was beaten with rods by the Romans. Once I was stoned by my enemies. Three times I was shipwrecked. I have spent a night and a day in the open sea. On frequent journeys, I faced dangers from rivers, dangers from robbers, dangers from my own people, dangers from the Gentiles, dangers in the city, dangers in the open country, dangers on the sea, and dangers among false brothers; labor and hardship, many sleepless nights, hunger and thirst, often without food, cold, and lacking clothing (2 Corinthians 11.24-27 HCSB).

That list is truly humbling and makes me reflect much on life and simply understand that my difficulties are nowhere near Paul's. However, our life difficulties are still our difficulties. Some scholars believe that Paul was small in stature, if that was the case then his height was overshadowed by his giant life. Equipped with brilliant intellect, a sensitive heart, tenacious drive, laser focus, and an intimacy with Christ like only a few. Paul kept going in his life's calling of being the apostle to the Gentiles.

Paul understood the exchanged life, that he was bought with a price,[14] and that Christ was living powerfully in Him to accomplish God's purposes.[15] In the book of Acts chapter 14 we find a short account that perfectly describes Paul's perseverance in his life's calling. In Lystra (a city in modern-day Turkey), after God through Paul healed a man who was lame from birth, the people mistakenly started treating Paul and Barnabas as gods. Paul and Barnabas couldn't get them to stop. Some Jews came rallied up the crowd to the point that they "stoned Paul, they dragged him out of the city, thinking he was dead" (Acts 14.19).

Paul got up and went back into the city! Afterwards, Paul and others preached in other towns and then went back to Lystra again! Oh, what he wouldn't do for the gospel of the risen Lord Jesus! He was compelled by the love of Christ to persevere, the world had to know that the prophesied Messiah had come and that there was a way to God. Paul knew that his momentary affliction was producing an incomparable weight of glory in the age to come.[16] With that insight nothing was going to stop him.

James Stalker, in his classic work *The Life of St. Paul*, describes how Paul was one of God's instruments who was used to accomplish some of God's mission to save humanity:

> He [Paul] gave his heart to the Gentile mission, and the history of his life is the

---

[14] 1 Corinthians 6.20; 7.23.

[15] Galatians 2.20.

[16] 2 Corinthians 4.17.

history of how true he was to his vocation. There was never such singleness of eye or wholeness of heart. There was never such superhuman and untiring energy. There was never such an accumulation of difficulties victoriously met and of sufferings cheerfully borne for any cause. In him Jesus Christ went forth to evangelize the world, making use of his hands and feet, his tongue and brain and heart, for doing the work which in His own bodily presence He had not been permitted by the limits of His mission to accomplish.[17]

May God grant us the grace that we desperately need so that we don't give up, so we finish what He has called each one of us to do knowing that the hour is late.

God's Grace

God's grace is a mystery. Every Pauline letter starts and ends with grace being directed toward the recipients. Anybody who has ever lived has experienced God's common grace: the normal care, love, and everyday providence from which God sustains the universe. Everybody who has ever been saved, has been saved by God's grace, His special prevenient efficacious grace, and

---

[17] James Stalker, *The Life of St. Paul* (Westwood: Revell, 1950), 17.

anybody who continues in the faith continues by the same God-given persevering grace.

God's grace is rightly understood as His unmerited favor toward undeserving sinners, but the concept of God's grace is so vast that it can't be fully described, albeit, A. W. Tozer is a great help in giving a working definition of God's grace:

> [The] Grace [of God] is the good pleasure of God that inclines Him to bestow benefits upon the undeserving. It is a self-existing principle inherent in the divine nature and appears to us as a self-caused propensity to pity the wretched, spare the guilty, welcome the outcast, and bring into favor those who were before under just disapprobation. Its use to us sinful men is to save us and make us sit together in heavenly places to demonstrate to the ages the exceeding riches of God's kindness to us in Christ Jesus.[18]

God's grace is what saves us, keeps us, and strengthens us so that we can persevere in this life no matter what we're experiencing. It brings God pleasure to see His people overcome, so God lovingly and generously dispenses His grace in special ways in just the right measure and at just the right time.

---

[18] A. W. Tozer, *The Knowledge of the Holy* (New York: HarperCollins, 1961), 93.

Olympian Ryan Hall, the fastest American half-marathoner ever (59:43) and the only American runner of a sub 2:05 Boston Marathon, made God his coach and through that faith-based coaching season learned much of God's grace. Hall witnesses to God's timely deliverance of grace and its connection to endurance as he writes, "Grace for the moment is the key to endurance. Grace is the supernatural power given by God to overcome in a situation, and the one who gives us this grace, Jesus, is right in front of us, in whatever moment we are in."[19]

God's grace is His supernatural power and kindness dispensed to the believer and ultimately has its origin in the person of Jesus. Grace is administered to the believer through Jesus. Jesus is the key, Jesus is the way, Jesus is the One who delivers this grace. Through Him we can persevere. The Bible records that grace is found in Jesus, grace came through Jesus, and grace and truth find their fulfillment in Jesus.[20] In essence, we need more of Jesus to persevere toward victory. No matter what happens to us in our life, to our loved ones, to our nation, to our world, let us say "Thanks be to God, who gives us the victory through our Lord Jesus Christ!"[21]

---

[19] Ryan Hall, *Run the Mile You're In: Finding God in Every Step* (Grand Rapids: Zondervan, 2019), 121-2.

[20] 2 Timothy 2.1; John 1.17; John 1.14 respectively. In a special way God's grace came through Jesus, but God's grace has been with people before Jesus' advent as seen in Genesis 6.8 with Noah and with Moses in Exodus 33.17, both found favor (grace) with God.

[21] 1 Corinthians 15.57.

Summary

We should never give in and we should always push on toward victory no matter what. By understanding that we have to persevere with endurance by the grace of God that is found in Jesus, and shifting our life's focus to God's purposes which always involve people, we can be victorious like the apostle Paul who went through much and never gave up. In some of the following chapters we'll apply Paul's experiences and see how meaningfully relevant they are to our lives. No matter what God allows us to experience in our life's journey, never, never, never, never - in nothing, great or small ever give up. Yes, life is hard, but by God's grace we'll persevere!

PAIN, DON'T GIVE UP

At the Mayo Clinic in Rochester, Minnesota, I encountered a man, Jean d'Aire. I stared at him. I stared intently. I stared as I thought about him. I just stared. He stood there in his bronze skin looking straight ahead, his muscular body hunched slightly forward with both hands loosely fist. His hollowed eyes were filled with pain. Heart pain, soul pain, his pain, our pain.

Auguste Rodin (1840-1917), the French sculptor who also carved The Thinker, sculpted Jean d'Aire. The sculpture is part of a monument to 'The Burghers of Calais' of the 14th century who offered themselves to King Edward III of England to spare their town. The first study of Jean d'Aire is the one described above. It speaks of persevering strength through pain and suffering. If you ever have the opportunity to meet Mr. d'Aire you'll know what I mean.

I think that many of us understand that life is filled with pain, may this section be an encouragement as we persevere through it.

Pain's Universality and Its Origin

Scripture is filled with examples and pictures of pain; physical pain and heart pain.[22] Pain is so vast in the Bible that the idea of pain is translated using no less than ten words: pain, sorrow, affliction, distress, labor, anguish, are only some of the words used to describe the sense of suffering that has many causes. Those are just a few terms that depict dozens of vivid portraits of pain which speak to/about our human experience.

Pain is universal. The created order experiences pain. Romans 8.22-23a reads, "For we know that the whole creation has been groaning together with labor pains until now. And not only that, but we ourselves who have the Spirit as the firstfruits – we also groan within ourselves . . ." All that God created in six days groans in pain, both nature and people.

Nature's pain shows itself in groans of droughts, earthquakes, famines, floods, hurricanes, and other natural disasters. The planet itself is hurting as it witnesses sin running its course of destruction. It deeply groans in its pain.

Similar to God's grace the mystery of pain in general and human pain specifically is indeed a mystery. We can connect pain's origins to what happened in Genesis chapter 3, the Fall of humanity, when sin entered into the world and death through sin. At the beginning God's

---

[22] By the term *heart pain,* I include mental psychological and spiritual pain.

created order was very good.[23] There was no sin, no pain, and no death.

God commanded Adam, the representative of humanity, not to eat from the Tree of the Knowledge of Good and Evil, if he did eat then Adam would certainly die.[24] Being deceived by the Satan-empowered serpent both Adam and Eve disobeyed God and ate from the tree. Because God is holy and just, He dished out judgment.[25] God told Eve, "I will intensify your labor pains; you will bear children in anguish." God's judgment on Adam included the ground being cursed, painful labor all the days of his life, and ultimately physical death.[26] Intensification of pain, anguish, a cursed earth, painful labor, and death sums up what humanity has experienced since that day.

The death that resulted was both physical and spiritual. Our first parents' physical death occurred slowly like when a leaf falls from a tree, it doesn't grow dry and crumble instantly, but over time it does dry out and finally crumbles. It dies. In contrast, spiritual death was instantly devastating; fellowship with God was ruptured as a once perfect relationship between man and God was

---

[23] Genesis 1.31.

[24] Genesis 2.17.

[25] Before addressing Adam and Eve, God first pronounced judgment on the serpent in verses 14-15. Not only was the serpent cursed to the ground, but the serpent (Satan) was to be crushed by the seed of the woman known as the Messiah, Jesus of Nazareth. This is the first messianic prophecy in the Bible. It's a picture of hope and of God's mercy and grace toward humanity in the midst of the worst event in human history.

[26] Genesis 3.16-19.

destroyed and in dire need of reconciliation. This was the start of unredeemed mankind's alienation from God.

Because Adam and Eve chose to disobey God's command, they sinned against Him. In the words of R. C. Sproul, they committed cosmic treason against God. Sin is the ultimate cause of pain and death in our world. Romans 5.12 states, "Therefore, just as sin entered the world through one man [Adam], and death through sin, in this way death spread to all men, because all sinned."[27]

Sin and its consequent death affected the entire created order. Adam and Eve experienced deeply the horrible reality of pain and death. We also experience pain and death meaning that death has torn apart what belongs together for the exercise and enjoyment of love, joy, peace, and contentment. Our first parents' eyes were opened and they saw themselves dead to God, to each other, and to nature.[28] This is ultimately why we all experience in one way or another pain and death, more

---

[27] One may observe and think that since Eve also sinned with Adam, she too should be held accountable for sin entering the world. Eve was held liable as God also judged her in the garden of Eden. However, God held Adam solely responsible for allowing sin to enter into the world because he was humanity's federal head/representative. The headship of Adam is also seen when God called for and questioned Adam first after the Fall in Eden (Genesis 3.8-11) even though Eve sinned first. Additionally, for a view of Satan's rebellion read Isaiah 14 and Ezekiel 28 where the passages speak of the kings of Babylon and Tyre respectively. These passages are understood to refer to Satan because the texts go beyond correlating strictly to humans.

[28] Summarized from Gerard Van Groningen, "Fall, the" in *Evangelical Dictionary of Biblical Theology*, ed. Walter A. Elwell (Grand Rapids: Baker, 1996), 241.

pain, more death, deep pain, and deep death as we live in this fallen world.

Pain

Physical Pain

There are basically two types of pain, heart pain and physical pain. Not all physical pain is bad. Just ask Rich Froning, the four-time winner of the CrossFit Games. During those victorious seasons, Rich, the fittest man on the planet, felt lots of physical pain in his preparation to outperform other elite athletes and raise his hands in victory.[29] Not only Rich but anyone who endures hard workouts of various muscle groups and taxes the cardiovascular system to improve one's fitness will experience delayed onset muscle soreness (DOMS).

If overall feeling and looking better is the goal, then the person who keeps up with challenging exercise reaps its benefits, even if the benefits cost physical soreness. Simply put, the gains are worth the pain.

We all can understand voluntarily physical aches and pains, this section isn't about those. We're concerned with

---

[29] Rich Froning won the CrossFit Games from 2011- 2014 and he also helped his Team Mayhem win four CrossFit Team championships in 2015, 2016, 2018, and 2019, for a record total of eight first-place finishes. Perhaps what keeps Rich Froning going could be the meaning of Galatians 6.14, "But as for me, I will never boast about anything except the cross of our Lord Jesus Christ. The world has been crucified to me through the cross, and I to the world." This verse is tattooed on one side of Rich's torso.

involuntary unavoidable (and sometimes chronic) physical pain and sickness in our bodies.

The book of Job is heart-wrenching and thought-provoking. In the first two chapters, Job's family and livelihood are instantly wiped out and we find him covered from head to toe with gruesome boils. A faithful believer of the God of Heaven, a righteous man in God's eyes, Job "was a man of perfect integrity who feared God and turned away from evil."[30] God allowed Satan to cause destruction in Job's life. Job felt both heart and physical pain during this assault.

Like Job the faithful follower of the Lord, many of God's people have unavoidably suffered deep physical pain. One of those servants of God who suffered is Watchman Nee (1903-1972). This dear Chinese brother who blessed and challenged the Church through his speaking and writing came to Christ at the age of sixteen (1920).

Nee was diagnosed with tuberculosis in 1926 and told he only had a few months to live. Nee wrote:

> I was not afraid of death, I had peace in my heart. But that night, when I thought upon the work of God, I felt I should not die. I must put into writing what lessons I had learned from the Lord in the past years, so that they would not go to the grave with me. And thus did I prepare to write *The Spiritual Man*.[31] [By 1929

---

[30] Job 1.1, 8, and 2.3.
[31] "A Sketch of the Author's Life" in *The Finest of the Wheat: Volume One* (New York: Christian Fellowship Publishers, 1992),

Nee's health worsened] At night I woke up every five minutes. I perspired a great deal. My hearing was so poor that people had to put their mouths near my ears for me to hear. My voice got coarse. Death seemed to be imminent. Telegrams were sent to various places asking for prayers. Nothing seemed to happen. A sister who was a nurse saw me and wept, for she had seen many severely-ill patients but none worse than I. Probably it had become a matter of three or four days before I would die.[32]

Having deteriorating health Nee set himself right with God by confessing sins and examining himself as he was ready to die. But God, being rich in mercy had other plans for Nee. God granted Nee the faith to be healed. The Scriptures that sparked Nee's healing were used to instruct Nee to *stand* fast (2 Corinthians 1.24), to *walk* by faith (2 Corinthians 5.7), and a reminder that the righteous would *live* by faith (Romans 1.17). Watchman Nee did just that, by faith in God and in His word, Nee literally stood up, walked out of his dwelling, and lived by faith! This was the beginning of God's healing and Nee's victory over sickness!

In the early 1950s the Communist Chinese government

---

17. The three-volume book *The Spiritual Man* is one of the few books Nee actually wrote. Many of Nee's writings were compiled from his speaking ministry.
[32] Ibid.

arrested Nee and other fellow Christian workers, and Nee spent the rest of his days in Communist labor camps.

In 1972 in his final letter, written to his sister-in-law, Nee wrote about the last illness that he would suffer. "It is a disease, an organic disease." Knowing that he would soon die Nee continued, "Please do not worry, because I maintain my joy. I hope you will also take good care of yourself. May your heart be filled with joy."[33]

Filled with the joy of God, Nee died May 31, 1972 with a severe case of heart disease, an enlarged heart. "The Lord had healed his tuberculosis miraculously and instantaneously, but his heart disease was never cured." Regarding his healing of tuberculosis, Nee testified that he came to know that experience as *the healing* of the Lord, concerning his heart disease he came to know the Lord as *the Healer*.[34]

There have been so many others who have served the Lord who have been very sick, some the Lord healed, others He didn't. In his book on lament, *The Hidden Face of God*, Michael Card recalls three of his best friends that God didn't heal and all died of cancer in the same year. Card's dear nephew Daniel, who just turned eighteen, Card's friend and mentor Bible scholar William Lane, and Card's friend John Eaves.[35]

Like Michael Card, we could all probably list several people who had faith in the Lord while suffering immensely physically, that list may include ourselves.

---

[33] Ibid., 31.

[34] Ibid.

[35] Michael Card, *The Hidden Face of God: Finding the Missing Door to the Father Through Lament* (NavPress, 2007).

The physical suffering that many of us face directly or indirectly could be tremendous. It's the day in day out of raw unfiltered pain that just doesn't go away, joined by all the appointments, the surgeries, the supplements, the medications that all take their toll on us sooner than later.

So, we pray, we stay in prayer, we ask for prayer, we pray and anoint with oil for healing, we fast and pray, we confess sin and pray, we claim God's word of healing when we pray. We know God hears us. But nothing really happens. It seems like we're not being healed or we're not going to be healed. When these thoughts and/or realizations come they're usually connected with another type of pain, heart pain.

Heart Pain

We don't have to be physically ailing to experience heart pain. Generally speaking, all people may not experience involuntary physical pain, but all people do experience heart pain. Heart pain includes many types of sadness, heart aches, heart breaks, and griefs that are due to various life experiences and trials. Since the human heart is a composition of the mind, will, emotions, and conscience,[36] heart pain is the deepest type of pain that we can experience. It encompasses so much and at times is ineffable.

[36] Witness Lee, a disciple of Watchman Nee, offers a great discussion on the three parts (tripartite) of man: body, soul, and spirit (1 Thessalonians 5.23) which includes the heart as being a major contributor to our immaterial part. Lee includes many Scriptures to explain this. See Witness Lee, *The Economy of God* (Anaheim: Living Stream Ministry, 1968) chapters 5-8 and others.

This pain may come from realizing one's own dire health situation, or recognizing another's health struggle. It could also arise from experiencing some of life's dreadful occurrences of having a wayward child, a loved one who's addicted to destructive behaviors/habits, a close friend who's far from God, loss of a job, loss of a family member/friend, broken relationships, being deeply misunderstood, being depressed, trying your best but finding out your best is just not good enough, being concerned with the lostness of the people in the world, etc. All these circumstances and a million more are all causes of heart pain.

The Bible shows us that the deepest heart pains come because we're concerned about others. The apostle Paul was deeply concerned about the Galatians reaching spiritual maturity, "My children, I am again suffering labor pains for you until Christ is formed in you." Paul also had a profound unsettlement with unbelievers and their hostility toward Jesus, "For I have often told you, and now say again with tears, that many live as enemies of the cross of Christ." He displayed intense care and genuine love for the believers at Corinth, "For I wrote to you with many tears out of an extremely troubled and anguished heart – not that you should be hurt, but that you should know the abundant love I have for you."[37] From the bottom of his heart Paul truly cared about people.

The Lord Jesus being concerned about His people Israel's salvation showed passionate heart pain when He was rejected by unbelieving Israel as He lamented, "Jerusalem, Jerusalem! She who kills the prophets and stones those who are sent to her. How often I wanted to

---

[37] Galatians 4.19; Philippians 3.18; 2 Corinthians 2.4 respectively.

gather your children together, as a hen gathers her chicks under her wings, yet you were not willing!"[38]

One of the most beautiful scenes of displayed heart pain was when Jesus wept over the death of His close friend Lazarus. The shortest verse in any English Bible reads, "Jesus wept."[39] "See how He [Jesus] loved him!"[40] explains the Son of God's tears. Jesus approached this situation of death and human suffering with a heart filled to the brim with love and compassion for both the loss of His friend and for Lazarus' family members' bereavement and heart-breaking grief. May we reflect and follow our Lord's compassionate example when we weep with those who weep (Romans 12.15).[41]

Tears

Our Tears

Tears are an important byproduct of heart pain. Internal pains are expressed through external tears. Before

---

[38] Matthew 23.37.

[39] John 11.35.

[40] John 11.36. Some Bible commentators think that Jesus could have wept because of the people's lack of faith and other reasons. Jesus' weeping over people's lack of faith is certainly possible, but I think that the text itself explains the main reason that tears fell from Heaven through Jesus, Jesus loved his friend, "See how He loved him" explains much.

[41] In weeping with those who weep, a memory of visiting my mom (who was very sick with a terminal illness) comes to mind when she and her roommate deeply wept together over life situations. In their words they "had a good cry."

there were drops of rain there were human tears. Tears are the defining reality of living in a death-infested, fallen world.[42] When the heart's pain threshold is reached, the dam that holds back our tears is breached; we taste the eyes' salty elements. "The Bible was written in tears, and to tears it yields its best treasures" said Tozer. The more we live, the more we realize the truth of that statement.

Many of us can relate to the sons of Korah as they wrote, "My tears have been my food day and night . . ." We can also remember our own experiences that mimic Jeremiah's ". . . my eyes flow with tears . . ."[43] As we reflect on the pain that causes tears let us agree with Ken Gire, "Perhaps there are no greater windows of the soul than our tears."[44] Tears help purify us in more ways than we know, tears help launder the soul.

One of my favorite verses is Psalm 56.8, "You [God] Yourself have recorded my wanderings [misery]. Put my tears in Your bottle. Are they not in Your records?" As I write my eyes fill as I relate to God's truth of our human experience.

This verse tells us much about God's compassion and His understanding of our fragile hearts. Consider this, God sees and records our miseries, griefs, and pains that cause tears, He stores our tears in His bottle, and jots each one down. He sees, relates to, and captures each tear from the hearts of His children. This kind of love and compassion is from another world, Heaven.

---

[42] Card, *The Hidden Face of God,* 75.

[43] Psalm 42.3; Lamentations 1.16 respectively.

[44] Ken Gire, *Windows of the Soul* (Grand Rapids: Zondervan, 1996), 192.

As our pain and suffering shouldn't be wasted, the tears that spring from them shouldn't be wasted either because they are precious to God. Yes let us weep to and with each other, but more importantly let us weep in God's presence. Let us share our heart's pain with Him like we never have before. May these tender words pluck a heart cord:

> Oftentimes it is useless to cry to each other; but if one cries to God it is effective, since God sees one's tears and will hear one's prayer. Indeed, every drop of tears shed before God will be counted by Him – "Thou numberest my wanderings: put thou my tears into thy bottle; are they not in thy book?" (Psalm 56.8) Please note that such is the advantage of having tears before God.

> O sorrowful heart, if life makes you suffer, and you are pressed beyond measure, passing your days in misery, and weary in battling many problems, why not cry before God? Let me tell you, this will never fail. God will record the tears you shed each time. He will put them in His bottle, which means He will remember all your sufferings. Thank God, our tears do not fall to the ground and mix with the dust; rather they are stored in God's bottle of remembrance; for are they not

in His record-books? God will not forget;
He will always remember our tears.[45]

In the final analysis when all is said and done our tears will be gone. The prophet Isaiah spoke of a time when God wipes away tears.[46] The book of Revelation tells us when that time will occur. The wiping away of all tears will happen in Heaven when we are in God's glorious presence dwelling with Him!

> Look God's dwelling is with humanity, and He will live with them. They will be His people, and God Himself will be with them and be their God. He will wipe away every tear from their eyes. Death will no longer exist; grief, crying, and pain will exist no longer, because the previous things have passed away.[47]

This heavenly vision gives us the hope of being released from this world of sin, pain, and death. In God's presence, all of our tears, our grief, our crying, all of our pain and all death will be gone. Hallelujah!

---

[45] Watchman Nee, *Powerful According to God* (Richmond: Christian Fellowship Publishers, 2005), 99.

[46] Isaiah 25.8.

[47] Revelation 21.3-4. God also wipes the tears of tribulation saints in 7.17, the difference here is that chapter 21's wiping of tears takes place in Heaven's eternity and is accompanied with the banishment of pain and death.

Jesus' Tears

We touched upon some occasions when the Lord Jesus shed tears. There's another occasion that shows the profundity of His tears. We're allowed to witness our Lord Jesus in superior pain and anguish that none of us could imagine. The writer of Hebrews writes that while Jesus our High Priest was on this earth episodes like this took place:

> During His [Jesus'] earthly life, He offered prayers and appeals with loud cries and tears to the One who was able to save Him from death, and He was heard because of His reverence. Though He was God's Son, He learned obedience through what He suffered. After He was perfected, He became the source of eternal salvation for all who obey Him, and He was declared by God a high priest in the order of Melchizedek. (Hebrews 5.7-10)[48]

---

[48] This may have been in the garden of Gethsemane (olive oil press) recorded in Luke 22.42-44, where Jesus said, "Father if You are willing, take this cup away from Me – nevertheless, not My will, but Yours, be done. Then an angel from heaven appeared to Him, strengthening Him. Being in anguish, He prayed more fervently, and His sweat became like drops of blood falling to the ground." Jesus' stressful pain was so severe that He sweat blood. The sweating of blood due to incredible amounts of stress is a real condition called hematidrosis. Moments like these are holy.

Jesus, the man of sorrows who was familiar with suffering, knew that offering Himself as the sinner's substitute to reconcile us to God would cost Him His life on a cross. On that cross God made Jesus, the One who did not know sin, to be sin for us so that we might become the righteousness of God in Him.[49] The mental and heart anguish of Jesus' incredible work on our behalf placed Him in pure excruciating agony. Pain, anguish, tears, He truly experienced as He prepared Himself to perfectly follow the plan of eternal salvation for mankind. He was making the way to God, because He Himself is the Way to God.

As mentioned, the deepest heart pains come from concerning yourself with others, our Lord Jesus is the perfect example of this. Jesus showed His loving concern for us that He voluntarily took our place on the cross. "He stepped into the role of the Substitute, representing His people. He didn't lay down His life for Himself; He laid it down for His sheep. He is our ultimate Substitute."[50]

Jesus as our Savior and High Priest, saves us and intercedes for us. Jesus knew pain. He was "a man of suffering" (Isaiah 53.3), and it is precisely that suffering and perfect obedience in suffering (Hebrews 5.8) that make Him fit for His roles as Savior and High Priest. Just

---

[49] 2 Corinthians 5.21, this verse is known as the Great Exchange, the exchange of our evil sin for the pure righteousness of the Son of God. Praise is in order – *To Him who loves us and has set us free from our sins by His blood, and made us a kingdom, priests to His God and Father – the glory and dominion are His forever and ever. Amen!* Revelation 1.5-6.

[50] R. C. Sproul, *The Truth of the Cross* (Sanford: Reformation Trust, 2007), 70.

as Jesus learned obedience to the Father by doing God's will, we also learn obedience to Christ by doing God's will.[51]

As man, Jesus knows the pains we experience. He lived on this earth, walked, talked, laughed, cried, just as we do. As God, Jesus tenderly comforts and strengthens us to keep going. So as the God-man He understands our hurts and our pains, He truly and compassionately understands, His tears tell us so. Michael Card reflects:

> As God, Jesus *knows* the depth of each of these bottomless pools of grief. As man, He is able to bring up, call forth, perhaps not even be able to hold back – tears. His contemporaries heard Him break into weeping more than once. Through the Incarnation, the tear that was poised in the eye of the world found expression as it coursed down the dark cheek of Jesus' face.[52]

Don't Give Up

We've learned about pain and tears. Physical pain and heart pain. Our tears and Jesus' tears. I'm here to tell you in spite of life's pain and tears, don't give up! When our body hurts, our heart hurts, and we have tears in our eyes let's not give up. Let's remind ourselves of some major truths: in this life *we will have pain, suffering, and*

---

[51] *CSB Baker Illustrated Study Bible*, 2371.

[52] Card, *The Hidden Face of God,* 75.

trouble in this world, but pain is temporary, God is with us, and glorification is coming! That's why we don't give up!

One main way for us not to give up is to gain some understanding and meaning in our pain and suffering. I believe if we can find meaning in our pain, then we won't give up because we'll have a reason to continue fighting, praying, encouraging, believing, and hoping.

In her enlightening book, *Wounded Heroes,* Elizabeth Skoglund writes wisely about effective living by finding meaning in our pain. I believe her words speak to many:

> Effective living involves a focus on dealing with problems in a way which ultimately means transcending them and going beyond them, at least for a time, not eradicating them. We have certainly not been promised a rose garden; but then we have not been set down in the midst of thorns either. When we are realistic, we see life as having both pain and pleasure.
>
> When we view life from this vantage point we will cease to berate ourselves for being so unspiritual as to suffer. Instead, we will accept God's gift of inner joy and find happiness in living lives content in a task. Meaning will be found, not lost, in suffering. For although we try by all means to avoid pain, there are times when

> it cannot be eradicated. Then the best
> solution to handling that suffering is to
> find some meaning in it.[53]

And the best way to find meaning in our suffering is to ask God. I believe God will answer if we truly listen for His voice. We serve an all-wise God Who has purposes in His allowing of our experiences. He never deals with us harshly just to deal with us harshly, any idea like that can go in the garbage because that's not God's character. The Bible tells us plainly that we know that *all things work together for the good of those who love God and are called according to His purpose.*[54] Yes, *all things* include our pain. Ask God the "why" questions on your heart. Ask Him to help you understand what's going on. Ask Him to show you your pain's purpose. He may answer quickly or it may take time, be patient in the answer concerning your affliction.

If you're sick and in need of God's healing I urge you to keep praying, and have others pray for you in a biblical way for your healing. Don't give up until you're healed. The Lord is a divine healer. In the Gospels, our Lord Jesus healed everyone who asked. He never turned anyone away. They asked, He answered.

It's the same with heart pain. Ask Him to heal you of your hurts, of your heart aches, of your anguish, of your

---

[53] Elizabeth R. Skoglund, *Wounded Heroes* (Grand Rapids: Baker, 1992), 15. Skoglund examines many Christians who have dealt with pain, physical and/or heart pain. She included: Amy Carmichael, Isobel Kuhn, C. S. Lewis, Charles Spurgeon, and others.

[54] Romans 8.28.

painful thoughts, of anything else that has caused you pain. Ask Him to take your pain away. Cast your burdens on Him because He cares for you.[55]

Lastly, let us remember that yes God is indeed the Healer, the Great Physician, and that He is also extremely holy, He is in heaven and we are on earth. Sin separates us from God and His favor, sin may also keep us from being healed from our pain. If you're not experiencing God's deliverance from pain it may be a sin issue.[56] If so, then ask the Holy Spirit to search your heart for any unconfessed sin, any way that is not of Him. Once He shows you your sin, confess it to Him, and ask Him for the strength to repent and to sin no more.

St. Augustine was right when he said, "God had one son on earth without sin, but never one without suffering." Even so let us thank and praise Him in our suffering as we don't give up while finding meaning in our pain. May God give us His perspective while we sow our terrestrial tears that will reap celestial shouts of joy.[57]

---

[55] A helpful book covering different types of healing and approaches to healing is Francis MacNutt, *Healing* (Notre Dame: Ave Maria, 1999).

[56] There are many reasons why God may not heal. In *Healing*, Francis MacNutt briefly writes on twelve reasons why God may not heal.

[57] Psalm 126.5.

Summary

Life's filled with pain. Let us take our pain to the Lord as we ask Him to help us understand His purpose(s) which will guide us in finding meaning in our pain. Our tears are never wasted as we weep in the Lord's presence. Though we may taste painful tears, don't give up.

PRESSURE, DON'T GIVE UP

As followers of Messiah Jesus, we sense many pressures in this world that desire to crush us. Out of the plethora some main pressures are to conform to/accept the ways of this wicked world, and the pressure to doubt God's word which leads to the pressure for us to be lukewarm Christians. As we live in the final stages of the Church age, these pressures and their intensity are forcefully increasing. God's word reminds and encourages us, "We are pressured in every way but not crushed."[58] God faithfully sustains us so we don't give up.

The Pressure of the Wicked World System

The best way to define most of main stream news is that it's media mayhem. The majority of news stories are filled

---

[58] 2 Corinthians 4.8a.

with sin and its consequences. Yes, this is the world in which we live. God's creation at the beginning wasn't like this, it was very good, fast forward thousands of years and we find ourselves in a chaotic existence.

This shouldn't surprise us too much because God's word tells of the heart-breaking reality of difficult times in the last days as people will be: lovers of themselves, lovers of money, boastful, prideful, blasphemers, ungrateful, unholy, generally unloving, slanderers, brutal, sexually immoral, without love for what is good, reckless, conceited, lovers of pleasure instead of lovers of God, satanic, nonsensical with darkened minds. People will have no self-control, they will claim to be wise but really be fools, they will destroy/degrade their own bodies, and they will exchange the truth of God for a lie as they worship the creation instead of God the Creator.[59]

We are witnessing all the above, we also see people being filled with unrighteousness, evil, greed, wickedness, envy, murders, quarrels, while being God-haters, arrogant, inventors of evil, disobedient to parents, undiscerning, untrustworthy, and unmerciful. As troublesome as that is people who act this way are found to be applauded in our society.[60]

The last two paragraphs describe our day regarding the people who are caught up in the wicked world system. First John 2.15-17 gives direction as it explains some of the system known as *the world*:

---

[59] See 2 Timothy 2 and Romans 1.
[60] Romans 1.28-32.

> Do not love the world or the things that belong to the world. If anyone loves the world, love for the Father is not in him. For everything that belongs to the world – the lust of the flesh, the lust of the eyes, and the pride in one's lifestyle – is not from the Father, but is from the world. And the world with its lust is passing away, but the one who does God's will remains forever.

The world system that we are talking about is an evil organized earthly system controlled by the power of Satan that has aligned itself against God and His kingdom purposes.[61] The pressure to accept and conform to this world system is tremendous. The persuasion to partake of this carnival of carnage assaults the faithful believer daily. It's a constant battle. A non-stop war that seeks to destroy God's witness and His true witnesses.

God gives a clear command to His people: *DO NOT LOVE THE WORLD OR THE THINGS IN THE WORLD.* This is not God's suggestion; this is a direct order. After God's command to not love the world, a logical material conditional is given stating that *if* anyone loves this world system *then* they don't love the Lord.[62] This is a warning from God telling believers to not love

---

[61] Daniel L. Akin, *1, 2, 3 John*, vol. 38 of *The New American Commentary* (Nashville: B&H, 2001), 108.

[62] A valid material conditional carries the idea of implication meaning if X is true then Y is true.

this world system, if they do love the world then they don't love the Lord.

Three major evils make up much of the world system: the lust of the flesh, the lust of the eyes, and the pride of one's life. The lust of the flesh is within and points toward our sinful nature, these lusts are the evil desires within one's self. The lust of the eyes comes from without, the things that we see arouse evil desires that one wishes to fulfill. There is much that enters our minds through our eyes. We see what is sensual and we want it, we see what is powerful and we want it, we see what we think will bring us fulfillment and we want it. The pride of one's life is arrogance or haughtiness about one's possessions, accomplishments, and/or social position(s).[63]

This world system that's filled with lustful evil people who are enticed by demonic forces is transient, it's passing away. A new age is coming where Jesus the Messiah will rule righteously for one thousand years and then eternal heaven will follow. However, before we get there, God's people are pressured to act like the world, follow the ways of the world, and to conform to it.

Be part of the crowd. Be part of the sheep that are asleep. "Just do you." "Do what you feel like doing" they tell us, or as Henley's *Invictus* proclaims to generations that are hell bound, "I am the master of my fate, I am the captain of my soul." These are all lies that confront the remnant believer. The whispers of this world are loud lies to the discerning soul. The attractions and fashions are all

---

[63] M. Rydelnik and M. Vanlaningham, eds., *The Moody Bible Commentary* (Chicago: Moody, 2014), 1978.

Satan's distractions. They are used to pressure us so that we don't get involved with God and His eternal purposes.

The Pressure to Doubt God's Word

The pressure to doubt God's word, the Bible, also comes from the world. From liberal theologians, so-called pastors, academics, History Channel shows, National Geographic films, social media vlogs, blogs, etc., the attack upon God's word and its truthfulness is tremendous. There are tons of great resources written by a multitude of scholars that clearly explain and defend the accuracy, veracity, and historicity of God's word.[64] Yet, the attack on the Bible continues. This isn't an apologetic for the truthfulness of God's word, I'm simply sharing my heart concerning what I deem as the pressure being applied upon us to doubt God's sixty-six volume love letter.

The Bible describes and explains our origins, gives us meaning, shows us where morality came from, and shows humanity's final destiny. The Bible is the most famous book of all time and it talks about the most famous person of all time, Jesus of Nazareth the Messiah, humanity's one and only Savior. The Bible has been proven to be reliable historically, archaeologically, and prophetically. No other

---

[64] Some helpful resources include: Norman L. Geisler and William E. Nix, *From God to Us: How We Got Our Bible* (Chicago: Moody, 2012), and S. B. Cowan and T. L. Wilder eds., *In Defense of The Bible* (Nashville: B&H Academic, 2013). A helpful resource of general Christian evidences is Josh McDowell and Sean McDowell, *Evidence That Demands a Verdict* (Nashville: Thomas Nelson, 2017).

book in the world has given prophecies that have come to pass. No other book in the world tells us about where we are on God's timeline and what is coming in the future, only the Bible.

Concerning future things, it seems that Christians are finding it hard to truly believe a couple orthodox Scriptural teachings, God's judgment on unbelievers and Jesus' Second Coming.

Jesus' Judgment on Unbelieving Humanity[65]

It's inevitable that the wickedness that we're currently witnessing/experiencing will ultimately be dealt with. Our society generally doesn't believe God's word, let alone His specific words concerning the final judgment that's coming. Whether people believe the Bible or not makes no difference in God's economy. Everything God has planned will take place just as it has been taking place, this includes future judgment by Jesus the righteous Judge.

Aside from Jesus being our Prophet, Priest, and King, He's also humanity's Judge. God the Father has given all judgment to Jesus the Son of God the Son of Man.[66]

---

[65] This section deals with the judgment of unbelievers. Believers will not be judged, but will be rewarded/or not rewarded at the Beyma (tribunal) seat of Christ. This is the place where believers will be evaluated on their stewardship of God-given talents, abilities, and responsibilities. See 2 Corinthians 5.10; Romans 14.10-12; 1 Corinthians 3.12-15.

[66] The Son of Man is a messianic title from Daniel 7.13. In John 5.27 God the Father has given all judgment to Jesus because He is the Son of Man, the Messiah. Son of Man used in the Gospels

Scripture illustrates this: "The Father, in fact, judges no one but has given all judgment to the Son" "He [Jesus] is the One appointed by God to be the Judge of the living and the dead" "He [God] has set a day when He is going to judge the world in righteousness by the Man [Jesus] He has appointed," it is "Christ Jesus, who is going to judge the living and the dead."[67]

The time and place where Jesus will judge unbelievers is after His 1000-year millennial reign on earth at the Great White Throne described by John in Revelation 20.11-15:

> Then I saw a great white throne and One seated on it. Earth and heaven fled from His presence, and no place was found for them. I also saw the dead, the great and the small, standing before the throne, and books were opened. Another book was opened, which is the book of life, and the dead were judged according to their works by what was written in the books.
>
> Then the sea gave up its dead, and Death and Hades gave up their dead; all were judged according to their works. Death

could also relate to the fact that Jesus is the only sinless perfect human, thus, by Jesus being the only perfect human He is suited to perfectly judge all fallen humanity.

[67] John 5.22; Acts 10.42, 17.31; 2 Timothy 4.1 respectively. There are more Scriptures that make this clear: Matthew 25.31-32; Romans 2.16; 2 Thessalonians 1.7-10; 2 Timothy 4.8; Revelation 19.11-16, 22.12, etc.

and Hades were thrown into the lake of fire. This is the second death, the lake of fire. And anyone not found written in the book of life was thrown into the lake of fire.

The throne is described as "great" and "white." It's great due to its enormous size compared to any throne in Revelation 20.4, great describes the One who occupies the throne, and great correlates to the significance of the judgment that stems from this throne. It's white because of the purity of the Holy One who sits on the throne, it shows the equity of justice that will be dispensed, and white also connects with the righteousness of the Judge and His verdicts.[68]

The dead being judged are all the unbelievers of all time. Social, financial, familial, or any other worldly status doesn't count here, *all* unbelievers will be judged. This is the day of reckoning that is coming in which every thought, motive, and action will be judged. "For God will bring every act to judgment, including every hidden thing, whether good or evil."[69] Everything in an unbeliever's life will be exposed and examined, nothing will be hidden from the piercing holiness of Jesus.

Aside from how an unbeliever lived, individuals will be primarily judged according to his/her response to Jesus. One of the most popular Bible verses is John 3.16, a

---

[68] E. Hindson, M. Hitchcock, and T. Lahaye, eds., *The Harvest Handbook of Bible Prophecy* (Eugene: Harvest House, 2020), 143.
[69] Ecclesiastes 12.14.

text full of God's grace and direction unto salvation, but the sad thing about many people knowing John 3.16 by heart is that most people don't know the two verses that follow. John 3.16-18 reads:

> For God loved the world in this way: He gave His One and Only Son, so that everyone who believes in Him will not perish but have eternal life. For God did not send His Son into the world that He might condemn the world, but that the world might be saved through Him. Anyone who believes in Him is not condemned, but anyone who does not believe is already condemned, because he has not believed in the name of the One and Only Son of God.[70]

True saving belief in Jesus will keep anyone from meeting Jesus as Judge. Once a person places saving faith in Jesus their name is written in God's book of life.[71] They will not experience Jesus as Judge at the Great White Throne followed by the hellish repercussion of being thrown into the Lake of Fire forever.

---

[70] John 3.36 also makes this point, "The one who believes in the Son has eternal life, but the one who refuses to believe in the Son will not see life; instead, the wrath of God remains on him."
[71] Daniel 12.1; Luke 10.20; John 5.24; Philippians 4.3; Hebrews 12.23; Revelation 3.5, etc.

Jesus' Return[72]

Jesus' judgment on unbelieving humanity is a consequent of His Second Coming (Gk. *Parousia*). Jesus' second coming/advent is the most prominent doctrine in the Bible second only to salvation. Prophecy scholar Mark Hitchcock writes, "There are 260 chapters in the New Testament and over three hundred references to the second coming of Christ. Jesus referred to His coming about twenty times, and His followers are commanded nearly fifty times to be ready for His coming."[73] Another prophecy expert, Paul Lee Tan, puts the eminence of Jesus' return this way:

> Time and again, the Bible describes the second coming of Christ. One out of every 30 verses in the New Testament repeats it. And one out of every 18 verses in the Old Testament points to it. If Christ had given this promise of His coming only once, that would have been enough. But the

[72] I will not address the Rapture and the Second Coming as two different events or the Rapture being the first phase/stage of the Second Coming in this section. My intent is to remind the believer that Jesus is indeed returning. For a defense of a pre-tribulation rapture being the first phase/stage of Christ's return see Ed Hindson and Mark Hitchcock, *Can We Still Believe in the Rapture?* (Eugene: Harvest House, 2017) and John Macarthur and Richard Mayhue eds., *Christ's Prophetic Plans* (Chicago: Moody, 2012). For a solid general resource on Bible prophecy see J. D. Hays, J. S. Duvall, and C. M. Pate, *An A-to-Z Guide to Biblical Prophecy and the End Times* (Grand Rapids: Zondervan, 2007).

[73] Mark Hitchcock, *The End: A Complete Overview of Bible Prophecy and the End of Days* (Carol Stream: Tyndale, 2012), 384.

> very fact of its being repeated some 4,200
> times in the Bible makes it a revelation
> which cannot be ignored.[74]

Scripture is clear that Jesus is returning. His return can be thought of from at least five perspectives: its being personal, physical, visible, unexpected, and triumphantly glorious.[75] The same Jesus that went up in a cloud on the Mount of Olives in Acts 1 is the same *personal* Jesus that will come back. Two angels said to the disciples, "This [same] Jesus, who has been taken from you into heaven, will come in the same way that you have seen Him going into heaven."[76] Within the same verse we see Jesus' second coming being *physical* in nature. Even though Jesus is always spiritually with us[77] He is coming back in His glorified resurrected body.

Jesus' second coming will also be *visible* to the world. Matthew 24.30 says, "Then the sign of the Son of Man will appear in the sky, and then all the peoples of the earth will mourn; and they will see the Son of Man coming on the clouds of heaven with power and great glory." Revelation 1.7 records, "Look! He is coming with the clouds, and every eye will see Him."

In Matthew 24-25[78] Jesus gave a prophetic discourse in which He explained many signs that will take place

---

[74] Paul Lee Tan, *Jesus is Coming* (Dallas: Bible Communications, 2010), 71.

[75] These categories are from Millard J. Erickson, *Christian Theology* 2nd ed. (Grand Rapids: Baker Academic, 1998), 1194-7.

[76] Acts 1.11.

[77] Matthew 28.20; Colossians 1.27; 1 John 4.4, etc.

[78] Parallel passages are also found in Mark 13 and Luke 21.

before His coming so that people would have indicators to recognize that they're either in or close to the season of His return. He also said that no one knows the exact day or hour of His coming except God the Father.[79] Thus, the coming of Christ will have a season of signs but the exact time will be *unexpected* and will catch many off guard.

Millard Erickson writes, "Jesus' teachings suggest that because of a long delay before the second coming, some will be lulled into inattention (Matt. 25:1-13; cf. 2 Peter 3:3-4). When the Parousia finally occurs, however, it will happen so quickly that there will be no time to prepare (Matt. 25:8-10)."[80] Jesus' return is likened to a thief in the night that catches people off guard showing that they were unprepared.[81]

Lastly, Jesus' return will be *triumphantly glorious*! Revelation 19.11-16 describes this resplendent event:

> Then I saw heaven opened, and there was a white horse. Its rider is called Faithful and True, and He judges and makes war in righteousness. His eyes were like a fiery flame, and many crowns were on His head. He had a name written that no one knows except Himself. He wore a robe stained with blood, and His name is the Word of God. The armies that were in heaven followed Him on white horses, wearing pure white linen. A sharp sword

[79] Matthew 24.36.
[80] Erickson, *Christian Theology*, 1196-7.
[81] Matthew 24.43; 1 Thessalonians 5.2.

came from His mouth, so that He might strike the nations with it. He will shepherd them with an iron scepter. He will also trample the winepress of the fierce anger of God, the Almighty. And He has a name written on His robe and on His thigh:

KING OF KINGS AND LORD OF LORDS

Heaven will open and release the majestic King Jesus as all creation see their regal Creator coming to earth! Starting at heaven's gates and coming through the clouds Jesus will eventually place His feet once again on the Mount of Olives in Jerusalem, which is the same location He ascended from forty days after His resurrection. This will fulfill the words of Zechariah 14.4.

There will be many occurrences that take place at Jesus' second coming, here are a few key events: Jesus will be in a final battle on earth against the Antichrist and his evil forces, Jesus will stand on the Mount of Olives as ultimate victor, Jesus will judge the nations and the Jews, and the marriage supper of the Lamb (the Bride/Church and Jesus) will occur.[82] Soon after these events take place Jesus' millennial kingdom will begin.[83]

---

[82] Some verses referring to each event: the final battle known as Armageddon (Habakkuk 3.13; 2 Thessalonians 2.8; Zechariah 14, etc.), Jesus standing victorious on the Mount of Olives (Zechariah 14.3-4), Jesus judging the nations and the Jews (Matthew 25.31-46; Ezekiel 20.34-8), and the marriage supper of the Lamb (Revelation 19.7-9).

[83] For helpful breakdowns of end time events chronology see: Arnold G. Fruchtenbaum *The Footsteps of the Messiah*, Ron Rhodes

The last time the unbelieving world saw Jesus was when He was crucified on a Roman cross. The situation will be completely different when He returns. Jesus is returning in glory, great power, and in judgment upon His enemies. He isn't coming back as a meek sacrificial Lamb like He came the first time; He's returning like a roaring Lion that will rule forever as every knee bows unto His holiness while all creation proclaims *Jesus is Lord!*[84]

Don't Give Up

The pressures of worldliness and to doubt God's word concerning the coming judgment and Jesus' return is turning many Christians lukewarm. This is heart breaking and alarming. I hope to encourage you *not to give up being a true servant of the Lord Jesus and to keep being a believing believer!* The Lord and His word are true. Judgment is coming on this wicked world and Jesus is returning soon! The reason it hasn't happened yet is because God is patient, willing that no one should perish but that all come to repentance (2 Peter 3.9). I tell you this much Jesus' coming is very near, closer than it was yesterday. Our world is crazy and will get crazier. Nevertheless, this is a season to be strong in the Lord and in the power of His might so that we don't give up; I recommend two key things that we do so that we don't.

The End Times in Chronological Order, and Leon J. Wood *The Bible & Future Events.*

[84] Philippians 2.10-11.

The Narrow Road

The first key item that must be done so that we don't give up is to freshly remember that we're called to live on/follow the narrow road. We mustn't forget for one moment that Christians are called to follow the Lord Jesus and not the ways of the world and its lies. Jesus said:

> Enter through the *narrow* gate. For the gate is *wide* and the road is *broad* that leads to *destruction*, and there are *many* who go through it. How *narrow* is the gate and *difficult* the road that *leads to life*, and *few find it* (Matthew 7.13-14, writer's emphasis).

Jesus tells us that the road unto salvation is narrow, and that the road to hell is broad. He tells us that few find salvation, and that many go to hell. Jesus tells us that the narrow road is difficult to live on, and the implication is that the broad road to hell is an easy/worldly even a superficial religious lifestyle. The narrow way of following Jesus and His words is the narrow road that leads to eternal life.

Following Jesus on the narrow road is not for the faint of heart. It's not an easy belief system that allows worldly living while placing Jesus and His purposes on the backburner. We must make a daily decision of whom do we serve, do we serve King Jesus the Lover and Savior of our souls or do we serve Satan and his demonic influenced world system? We must decide.

I fully believe Jesus' words that only few find eternal life, meaning that compared to all the people who ever lived there were/are relatively few who are saved, possibly only 25 percent. Let me explain, in the Parable of the Sower found in Matthew 13.1-9 explained in 13.18-23, Jesus describes four types of soil/people who hear the word of God (the Gospel) and their general responses.

There are three negative responses and one positive. The negative responses to the Gospel include that: the word is ate up or destroyed by Satan/demonic influences, the word withers because of pressure or persecution, and the word is choked by being caught up in the world system. The only positive response to the word of God is that it was productive.

This is God's illustration of four types of people and their responses to the Gospel and the call to follow Jesus. Three out of the four eventually fell away, they got "ate up," they "withered," and they got "choked." Three out four is 75 percent. The 25 percent that is left are the true followers of Jesus that had fruitful/productive lives, these believers are described as being "good ground." They heard and understood the word, and were faithful unto Jesus and His purposes.

The point in being fruitful/productive is not doing everything and being involved in a million ministries. No, I believe the main point is faithfulness unto Jesus and right stewardship of our God-given talents, abilities, and responsibilities in whatever He has called each one of us to do. God is all-wise as He has already coordinated good works for us to be involved in (Ephesians 2.10).

He places us in certain times at certain places to be His faithful witnesses.

Back to the narrow road. Are we part of the few? Which road are we on? The narrow? The broad? Is there some confession of sin and repentance that must take place to get back on Jesus' narrow road? Time is running out.

We must understand that most professing Christians are lukewarm, these are the ones that Jesus said that He would vomit out of His mouth because they make Him sick. This may be a hard pill to swallow but Jesus Himself said it.[85] He means business, He's not playing around. He died and rose for us, are we living faithfully for Him? We are His instruments to reach the lost, are we reaching? We are supposed to be the salt that helps delay world decay, are we godly salt? We are supposed to be His vessels of love, mercy, grace, and truth to the people in this world, are we?

Let us acknowledge that worldly people are going to do what worldly people do. Let us acknowledge that lukewarm Christians are going to be lukewarm Christians. Let's not be part of this worldly system and lukewarm Christianity, this is not God's will for us. We will never be overcomers who live victorious lives if we follow the worldly broad road that leads to destruction.

Continuing Pressure

The second key item that must be done to persevere unto victory is to come to the realization that the pressure to be part of the godless world system, to doubt God's

---

[85] Revelation 3.16.

word, and to live as a lukewarm Christian is never going to stop. As long as we live in this fallen world it will continue. As Paul and other Christians were constantly pressured from all sides as they were living faithfully in their callings, the same is going to happen to any true disciple. However, the key is to realize that as Paul and others felt constant pressure, they were never crushed because God was with them protecting them and strengthening them.

Paul knew that he was as fragile as a clay jar as he shared the treasure of the Gospel. He also knew that God would grant him and any other believer extraordinary power to be faithful to God's will. That's why Paul said, "We are pressured in every way but not crushed" (2 Corinthians 4.8). In essence, we do our part and serve God under pressure, and God does His part to protect us from not being crushed by it. In this way we participate with God in His purposes while His grace powerfully sustains us.

Let us seek Him for more of Him while He may be found. Let us ask the Holy Spirit to purify us from anything that is not of Him. Let us ask God to make Himself more real to us than He has ever been. Let us ask God to show His power to us. Let us believe God to do remarkable things that will encourage us. Let us ask Him to build our faith to the highest levels ever. Let us not give up asking, seeking, and knocking. We will receive, find, and doors will open that will lead to new levels of intimacy with Him and obedience to Him. Let us resolve in our hearts that we will serve Him no matter what type of pressures may come.

Summary

I'm certain that once we resolve in the presence of God to serve Him under any pressure, pressures will increase to try to crush us. Pressures from the world, lusts, and demonic influences. However, we'll never be crushed and give up because Jesus in us is greater than Satan who is in the world.[86] Let us resolve to stay close to Jesus as we follow Him as we stay alert looking for the blessed hope of His return. Jesus overcame the world, and by His grace, our faith, His blood, and our testimony so will we.[87]

---

[86] 1 John 4.4.
[87] John 16.33; 1 John 5.4-5; Revelation 12.11.

PERPLEXED, DON'T GIVE UP

This age in which we're living can be so confusing. The world bombards us daily with thousands of mixed signals and false destructive information that work in unison to simply confuse us in knowing the truth about what to believe, what to do, and how to live. This is not God's will.

Paul and other early Christians testified that as they served the Lord even they were perplexed (Gk. *aporeo*) at times, they were at a loss for what to do and how to continue (2 Corinthians 4.8). This chapter discusses three areas: world confusion, religious confusion, and life's confusion. God is not the god of confusion; He is the God of clear truth who wants us to be wise as we persevere while trusting Him.

Eloy Puga

World Confusion

Perplexed and words like puzzled, confused, mystified, and bewildered carry the same idea as the Greek word *aporeo*. Aporeo means to be without a way, without resources, in doubt, and at a loss not knowing what to do.[88] The Lord Jesus mentioned that people in this world would be at some level of confusion before His return. "Then there will be signs in the sun, moon, and stars; and there will be anguish on the earth among nations *bewildered* by the roaring sea and waves" (Luke 21.25, writer's emphasis). I believe that we're currently seeing a foreshadowing of Jesus' words.

The Bible is the deepest kind of literature that exists. It is inexhaustible. In God's wisdom He has related types in the Bible that give deeper meaning to certain passages. A type is a prophetic representation, one thing that prefigures another.[89] In biblical typology the sea represents restless humanity.[90] Jesus' words that the nations will be bewildered by the roaring sea and waves can be understood two ways, literally and symbolically.

Jesus spoke about the literal chaotic behavior of bodies of water known as seas in which the people of the nations will be confused by as they witnessed the seas' powerful strange movements before His return. The roaring of the

---

[88] James Strong, *The New Strong's Expanded Dictionary of Bible Words* (Nashville: Thomas Nelson, 2001), 980.

[89] Kevin J. Conner, *Interpreting the Symbols and Types* (Portland: Bible Temple,1992). Another helpful resource regarding biblical types is Walter L. Wilson, *Wilson's Dictionary of Bible Types* (Grand Rapids: Eerdmans, 1957).

[90] Isaiah 57.20; Jude 13.

seas can also be understood symbolically as representing the people of the nations as seen in Isaiah 57.20-21, "But the wicked are like the storm-tossed sea, for it cannot be still, and its waters churn up mire and muck. There is no peace for the wicked, says my God," in Jude 13 apostates are called *wild waves of the sea*, and in Revelation 13.1 the final Antichrist figure emerges from the sea (the nations).

As we apply this understanding to God's word it helps illuminate some of our current global situation's dark confusion. As the nations (restless humanity) are churned even more by the waves, let us understand that not all waves of the sea are equal, all contain salt water, but some also contain fallen angels.

Let me explain. Satan's and the fallen angels' main abode is the first heaven known as earth's atmosphere. The Bible says that there are ranks of angels that dwell in the heavens (Ephesians 6.12). In the first chapter of Job, we see that Satan used a storm and winds to bring destruction to Job's situation.[91] In Mark 4.39, Jesus rebuked the wind and the sea by commanding, "Silence! Be still!" One normally doesn't address impersonal objects, but personal ones. Jesus rebuked the fallen angels who were using winds and the sea attempting to destroy Jesus and His disciples.

After Jesus rebuked the fallen angels who used the wind and sea as weapons, part of the next scene's final act shows Jesus driving out 2000 demons called Legion into a herd of pigs that ran off a hillside into the sea of Galilee. Those demons who possessed the pigs are now in that body of water causing ruckus and have been ever since.

---

[91] Job 1.16,19.

So, when we read in Luke 21.25 that in the end times soon before Jesus' return the nations will be confused by the roaring of the sea and the waves, yes it means that powerful strange natural disasters will be increasingly occurring, but it's also showing deep workings of demonic forces among human affairs.

That's exactly what we are experiencing in our upside-down world right now; demonic influenced confusion on a global scale where falsehood is propagated as truth, truth is censored, and global social conditioning is happening.

Concerning global social conditioning that's taking place based on a lie, the COVID-19 plandemic is the deceptive tool that is being used to condition people for the One World system that's around the corner.[92] Think of it, within a single year's time people have been pumped 24 hours a day with the same unified false narrative that COVID-19 is a death sentence, when in reality according to the world's foremost epidemiologist, John Ioannidis (Stanford University), over 99.8% of the people who do truly get COVID-19 fully recover.[93]

The false narrative that COVID-19 is a death sentence has instituted so much blind fear that most people are uncritically taking orders from naïve godless governments and the activist media such as: stay home, wear a mask, six feet social distance, don't go to church, don't meet

---

[92] See appendix, *A Watchman's Unscientific Meditation of Reasonable Random Thoughts*.

[93] Dr. John Ioannidis "Infection Fatality Rate of COVID-19 Inferred from Seroprevalence Data" in *Bulletin of the World Health Organization* (October 14, 2020) https://www.who.int/bulletin/online_first/BLT.20.265892.pdf .

with people, don't go to work, take an unnecessary experimental gene-therapy "vaccine," etc. This is utter nonsense. Pam Popper and Shane Prier, in their insightful and well documented work, *COVID Operation*, state and show that COVID-19 is the biggest hoax in world history.[94]

This global lie is undoubtedly connected with spiritual forces of darkness. It seems that the enemy has not only confused people with a lie to what's really going on, but more importantly the enemy keeps blinding people from the truth of the Gospel (2 Corinthians 4.4). Satan, the king of confusion and lies, who steals, kills, and destroys is working overtime with propagating confusing deception because he knows that his time is short before he and his fallen angels are thrown into the eternal Lake of Fire. Until then, he and his minions are the destructive deceivers on the loose that roaringly perplex the nations.

Religious Confusion

Apart from the global COVID plandemic that has caused much destruction and disorder there is also religious confusion, mainly the lies that there are many roads to God/salvation and the lie that everyone goes to heaven at death. The Bible does not teach such things, never hints at them, and is clear that the only way to God/salvation is through Jesus Christ of Nazareth, and that everyone does not go to heaven when they die.

---

[94] Pamela A. Popper and Shane D. Prier, *COVID Operation: What Happened, Why It Happened, and What's Next* (Self Published, 2020), 12.

The world having various religions is the reality of religious variety, not to be confused with religious pluralism. Religious pluralism is the idea that all/most religions lead to God/salvation. The lie of religious pluralism is one part of the spirit of the age that has been propagated full force through many outlets: religious, educational, entertainment, main stream media, social media, etc.[95] In contrast, religious exclusivism the idea that there is only one way/religion that leads to God/salvation is true. That truth is found in orthodox Christianity in the person of Jesus. Exclusive salvation through Jesus of Nazareth is what the Bible teaches.

In John 14.6, Jesus made it clear that He is the way, the truth, and the life, and that no one comes to God the Father except through Him (Jesus). In Acts 4.12, The Apostle Peter echoed the same exclusive claim that there is salvation in no one else except in Jesus, that there is no other name given by God to be saved through except Jesus, and that people must be saved through Jesus. Jesus is the exclusive way to salvation; He is the only way to God. God categorically gives no other option.[96]

---

[95] Religious inclusivism is another view within circles of Christianity, the basic idea is that Christianity is true, but God's grace is working through other religions and followers of those religions may still be saved anonymously, meaning that those religions' adherents do not need to place their faith in Jesus necessarily. This is a lie also. For biblical support of this view, one must perform interpretational gymnastics. In essence, religious inclusivism is an offshoot of religious pluralism's falsehood.

[96] Some helpful works on Jesus being the only way to God when compared to other religions/religious leaders are: Douglas Groothuis, *Are All Religions One?* (Downers Grove: Intervarsity,

By being the prophesied Jewish Messiah who fulfilled messianic prophecies,[97] Jesus is the only one qualified to be the world's Prophet, Priest, King, and Savior. The world needed a Savior and God sent one in Jesus. The world needed someone to pay the penalty of sin against holy God, Jesus paid the debt and is the believing sinner's propitiation. By paying the sin debt Jesus made the way so that we can be forgiven. Greg Koukl writes, "Jesus is the only source of salvation because there is no forgiveness possible unless Jesus died on the cross as payment. Jesus is the only object of salvation because we must believe on Him and none other for this forgiveness to be ours."[98]

No other religion/faith teaches that a person's sins must be forgiven to be reconciled to God, and that a person has to be spiritually born anew, only Christianity teaches these truths while offering forgiveness and eternal life through the God-man Jesus Christ. Jesus is the only way to God and He proved it remarkably by His resurrection.

1996), and Kenneth R. Samples, *God among Sages: Why Jesus Is Not Just Another Religious Leader* (Grand Rapids: Baker, 2017).

[97] https://reasons.org/explore/blogs/todays-new-reason-to-believe/read/tnrtb/2003/08/22/fulfilled-prophecy-evidence-for-the-reliability-of-the-bible

[98] Greg Koukl, *Jesus the Only Way: 100 Verses* (Signal Hill: Stand to Reason, 1995), 4. As Jesus paid the believer's sin debt, He was our substitute on the Cross, meaning either we ourselves pay the penalty of death for our sin, or someone else has to satisfy the wrath of Holy God against us; Jesus paid the sin debt as our substitute. If anyone says that Jesus did not take the role of substitute in the sinner's place, the person who makes that claim simply doesn't know the Bible, see Isaiah 53.5-6, 11-12; Matthew 20.28; John 1.29; 2 Corinthians 5.21, etc.

He is currently exalted at the right hand of God in heaven while simultaneously spiritually indwelling His followers.

Whether a person believes that Jesus is the only way to God or not doesn't change the truth that He is. This is objective unchanging truth. One may respond that truth is subjective/relative, however, truth doesn't change and isn't dependent upon our thoughts, feelings, or opinions. Truth is mind independent and connects with reality. Meaning that it doesn't matter whether or not someone believes the truth, likes the truth, thinks that the truth is false, etc., the fact is that reality still stands and will stand.

For example, we could be standing on a sea shore seeing a tidal wave 50 miles away headed toward us. We may choose to stay on the shore and tell ourselves over and over that we don't like tidal waves and we don't believe in them, but this won't change the reality that a tidal wave is coming, and if we don't move we'll be smashed by the wave's reality.

Another religious lie in our world that's permeated through society is what I call salvation by death. Salvation by death is the erroneous idea of universalism in which everybody goes to heaven. There seems to be a common (mis)understanding that when a person dies that soul passes automatically through heaven's gates. A person could've lived like a heathen and then died, and somehow people will say the deceased is in a "better place," or when a decent moral person dies likewise that person is ushered into heaven also.

If a person has not placed saving faith in Jesus Christ, then based on the authority of Scripture that person will certainly not be in heaven with God after death. No matter how wonderful, charitable, nice, smart, good-looking, rich, etc. that that person was, if they didn't have a genuine born from above personal relationship with Jesus before they died, then Jesus will tell them, "depart from Me I never knew you."[99]

I believe those two religious lies: the lie that Jesus is not the only way to God/salvation, and the lie that everyone goes to heaven when they die have been used by the enemy to confuse multitudes while sending them to hell.

Life Confusion, Don't Give Up

Life is not lived in black and white, there are many gray areas we encounter in which we just don't know what to do. We're at a loss, we tried everything, thought about ways to work things out, but we're just in a bind of confusion and we don't know what to do. We think to ourselves, "Should I call them or not?" "Which way

---

[99] John 3 is a clear chapter that teaches that a person must be born from above (regenerated - given spiritual life) to enter the kingdom of God. John 3.16-18 makes it clear that God offers eternal life in Jesus and if a person doesn't believe in Jesus then God's wrath remains upon them. See John 3.36 also. In Matthew 7.13-23, after Jesus teaches that there is a narrow road to eternal life, Jesus states that no matter how much activity (even religious) a person has performed, if one does not do the will of the Father then they will be cast away from God's presence. The main will of the Father is that a person believes in Jesus the Son (John 6.29). Lastly, John 1.12-13 teaches that a person must believe in Jesus to be a child of God. Faith in Jesus is the key to salvation. Lacking faith in Jesus leads to damnation.

should I go?" "Now what am I going to do?" Let me tell you from one perspective this is a good place to be. God is working. Give Him time to work. Trust Him, wait upon Him. One of the worst things we could do is take matters into our own hands when things aren't clear about the direction that we should proceed.

The Old Testament was given to us for many reasons, one reason is that God wants us to learn life lessons from the people who went before us.[100] If those examples turned out bad then we must learn from them, if the examples turned out well, then likewise we must learn from them also. God doesn't want us to learn everything from firsthand experience, He wants us to be wise, and in His wisdom He has given us many lessons in His word that we need to heed.

One person's example that we must learn from is from Israel's first king, Saul. Saul, the people's king, made a detrimental mistake that began his downfall. In 1 Samuel 13, the Philistines were approaching and Israel's soldiers started abandoning Saul. Previously Samuel told Saul to wait for him as Samuel would make an offering to God. Saul jumped the gun as he didn't wait long enough for Samuel and Saul decided to offer the burnt offering himself. "Just as he [Saul] finished offering the burnt offering, Samuel arrived. So, Saul went out to greet him, and Samuel asked, "What have you done?""[101]

This is such a sad moment. Saul had no right in taking a priestly position and to perform the offering, this was strictly Samuel's God-given duty. Samuel's question to

---

[100] 1 Corinthians 10.1-6.
[101] 1 Samuel 13.10.

Saul "What have you done?" speaks volumes. In Saul's anxious confusion about God's timing, Saul didn't wait on the Lord as he took matters into his own hands - a grave mistake. Samuel didn't mince words as he told Saul, "You have been foolish. You have not kept the command which the LORD your God gave you" (1 Samuel 13.13). May this word speak to our hearts.

I believe that most confusion we experience is because we don't trust God in waiting for Him. Dear brother/ sister what are you confused about? What in this season of life has bewildered you? Have you gone to your heavenly Father about your situation? Have you spent time in Jesus' presence telling Him about your perplexity?

When we're confused about life's situations, we must seek the Lord for clarity as we patiently wait on the Lord for His answer and direction. Loved and cherished one of God, may I speak bluntly with you, if you've truly sought the Lord for an answer, I believe that He has probably already answered you. You may not like His answer, but God is the God who answers His children when we call. His word says, "Call to Me and I will answer you . . ." (Jeremiah 33.3).

Like Saul being foolish and not waiting on the Lord as he went ahead and did things outside of God's perfect timing, I plainly tell you to stop being foolish and obey the Lord. Obey His word, obey what He has spoken through other people, through situations, through the many avenues that God uses to speak to us. Listen for His voice and obey. God's word tells us that to pay attention and obey is better than any sacrifice (1 Samuel 15.22).

Stop being so hesitant, renew your resolve to trusting and waiting on the Lord. Obey His word and you could be certain that it will go well for you. Just wait and see. He has your best interest at heart – all the time! Don't give up trusting Him to answer you; He will answer and bring you clarity.

Listen, I'm not confused about much these days. I study Bible prophecy and I see the way the world's heading; I see things being set up to fulfill God's prophetic words. I find deep comfort and encouragement that He's in complete control of world events – yes definitely, so I rest in the fact that He's perfectly handling the events in my life and yours too! He is God Almighty and I'm sure of this that He who started a good work in you will complete it until the day of Christ Jesus (Philippians 1.6).

Let us learn from Moses and the Israelites' Exodus Red Sea moment when all seemed lost as Pharoah and the Egyptians were on their tail chasing them down. God's people didn't know what to do or where to go. Through natural eyes it seemed like there was no hope for them, BUT GOD! He had already worked everything out in advance. Moses trusted in the Lord for deliverance, God Himself split the Red Sea and made a victorious way for His people. The key to victory is trusting God and waiting on Him in all the perplexing situations of life.

In God's grace, He has given many Psalms to help guide our lives. The 150 Psalms in the Bible touch on every aspect of our human experience. Psalm 25 is a beautiful Psalm to read and to obey when needing God's clarifying direction, may it be activated in your life by the Holy Spirit to encourage you to trust and to wait upon the Lord: "Lᴏʀᴅ, I turn to You. My God, *I trust in You*" (v.1-2). *"No one who waits for You will be disgraced . . . Make Your ways known to me, Lᴏʀᴅ; teach me Your paths. Guide me in Your truth and teach me, for You are the God of my salvation; I wait for You all day long"* (v.3-5). *"He leads the humble in what is right and teaches them His way"* (v.9). *". . . He [God] will show him the way he should choose"* (v.12). *"My eyes are always on the Lᴏʀᴅ . . ."* (v.15). "May integrity and what is right watch over me, for *I wait for You*" (v.21).

Summary

Yes, the world system sends confusion, but we don't have to be confused. Yes, religious lies abound that cause confusion, but we have God's word to trust in so we shouldn't be confused. Yes, life at times could be confusing, but *let us refuse to be confused*! God's word brings clarity out of all types of confusion. Let's not give up trusting, hoping, and waiting upon Him. God has spoken to us, we who trust/hope/wait upon the Lᴏʀᴅ will renew our strength; we'll soar on wings like eagles, we'll run and not grow weary, we'll walk and not faint![102]

It'll go well with us if we stop seeking worldly direction and worldly answers for many of life's situations in which we find ourselves. David Wilkerson has wise words to encourage us:

> Stop searching! Stop looking in the wrong direction for help. Get alone with

---

[102] Isaiah 40.31.

Jesus in a secret place; tell Him all about your confusion. Tell Him you have no other place to go. Tell Him you trust Him alone to see you through. You will be tempted to take matters into your own hands. You will want to figure things out on your own. You will wonder whether God is working at all; there will be no sign of things changing. Your faith will be tested to the limit. But nothing else works, anyway, so there is nothing to lose. Peter summed it all up: "To whom shall we go? Thou [Jesus] hast the words of eternal life" (John 6.68).[103]

---

[103] David Wilkerson, *Have You Felt like Giving Up Lately?* (Grand Rapids: Revell, 1980), 116.

PERSECUTION, DON'T GIVE UP

Persecution is certain. It's been foretold by Jesus Himself. He spoke about global persecution in the Gospels and in Revelation. It's inevitable. Jesus warned that many would fall away from the faith. If you are a born-again Christian you will face persecution, but you have God's higher help so don't give up.

Promised Persecution

Jesus said, "But before all these things, they will *lay their hands on you* and *persecute you,* they will *hand you over* to the synagogues and prisons, and you will be brought before kings and governors *because of My name. It will lead to an opportunity for you to witness*" (Luke 21.12-13).[104] There's a purpose in persecution. It's a wonderful opportunity to share Christ and the Gospel.

---

[104] All emphasis in this chapter is mine unless noted otherwise.

Jesus continued, "You will even be *betrayed* by parents, brothers, relatives, and friends. *They will kill some of you. You will be hated by everyone because of My name*, but not a hair of your head will be lost. *By endurance* gain your lives" (Luke 21.16-19).

In these verses Jesus tells us that some will be martyrs being put to death.[105] While Christian martyrs may die on earth they will live eternally with God. They will also reign with Christ on earth for 1000 years.

The condition of a martyr is reflected in this verse, "we are persecuted but not abandoned; we are struck down but not destroyed" (2 Corinthians 4.9). While Jesus will not keep us from persecution, He will be with us through persecution. He will never leave us nor forsake us. We are never alone.

Persecution is a part of Christian life if we live godly. You may say I'm not persecuted. May I ask you why not? Some of the Apostle Paul's last words were, "In fact, all those who want to live a godly life in Christ Jesus will be persecuted" (2 Timothy 3.12). If we witness in the Name of Jesus, we will face opposition and persecution. This is inevitable, a simple Bible truth.

In the beginning of this book, I referred to a powerful foe of God and of nations. Nazi Germany was attacking

---

[105] The word martyr means a person who has died for a cause. The word translated *witness* in many Bible translations is the Greek word for martyr. In Acts 1.8, Jesus said, "But you will receive power when the Holy Spirit has come on you, and you will be My *witnesses* (martyrs) in Jerusalem, in all Judea and Samaria, and to the ends of the earth." All the apostles died as martyrs. Traditionally, the apostle John died last in forced seclusion because of His testimony concerning Jesus.

many countries and was responsible for World War II. Their leader was the demonically controlled Adolf Hitler. Prime Minister Winston Churchill encouraged multitudes to press on and never give in. During the time of Hitler there were also Christians in Germany and we can learn from their persecution. Did they give in?

There were 14,000 German Evangelical pastors and their congregations. Hitler put pressure on the Christian Churches. It even went so far to where Hitler changed the Bible, removing a part, changing the commandments, and having parts of the New Testament re-written. He also demanded for the Churches to put the swastika into every Church. Hitler quoted Romans 13.1 to the Evangelical pastors and churches, "Everyone must submit to the governing authorities, for there is no authority except from God, and those that exist are instituted by God." Most pastors and Christians felt helpless in the midst of the storm. 13,200 Evangelical pastors and their congregations compromised with Hitler.

800 remnant pastors followed what Peter and John said to the religious establishment in Acts 4.19, "Whether it's right in the sight of God for us to listen to you rather than to God, you decide." 800 of Christ's undershepherds stood strong in Germany and followed God.

We're familiar with 6 million Jews having died in German concentration camps. Not many know that there were also 5 million others who died in concentration camps, including Christians who stood up for Christ. 800 pastors did not compromise as they remained true to the Bible. They went to prisons, concentration camps, and some to their death.

One of the leaders of the 800 was Pastor Martin Niemoeller, he wrote:

> First they came for the Socialists,
> and I did not speak out —
> Because I was not a Socialist.
>
> Then they came for the trade unionists,
> and I did not speak out —
> Because I was not a trade unionist.
>
> Then they came for the Jews,
> and I did not speak out —
> Because I was not a Jew.
>
> Then they came for me —
> and there was no one left
> to speak for me.[106]

Niemoeller survived, not all did. For his opposition to the Nazi state control of the churches, Pastor Niemoeller was imprisoned in the concentration camp of Sachsenhausen and then the concentration camp of Dachau near Munich from 1938 to 1945. He narrowly escaped execution and death.

Dietrich Bonhoeffer, another Christian leader against Hitler was initially sent to Tegel Prison in Berlin, then to Buchenwald concentration camp, and finally he was

---

[106] Martin Niemoeller, *First they came* . . . . This is one version of the poem, there's a longer version engraved at the New England Holocaust Museum in Boston, Massachusetts.

sent to Flossenbuerg concentration camp, where he was hanged.

After the second world war ended in 1945, Pastor Niemoeller led German Christians in a Stuttgart Declaration of Guilt. A declaration was issued on October 19, 1945 by the Council of the Evangelical Churches in Germany, in which they confessed guilt for their inadequacies in opposition to the Nazis and the Third Reich. The Declaration of Guilt states in part: *Through us infinite wrong was brought over many peoples and countries --- we accuse ourselves for not standing to our beliefs more courageously, for not praying more faithfully, for not believing more joyously, and for not loving more ardently.*

The signs of the times in North America tell us that a demonic war has been declared against the Word of God and the Churches of Jesus here in North America. You answer perhaps: We're still dealing with a pandemic in North America. What can we do? O you of little faith, the Lord told us: The weapons of our warfare are not carnal but mighty in God.[107] The German Christians stated some of the weapons of spiritual warfare: courageous and joyous faith, faithful prayer, and ardent love. Now is the time to wake up and wield such weapons.

"The early church was marked with suffering, persecution, peril, and rejection. The modern church knows nothing of these majestic scars. Instead of entering into the sufferings of Christ, we have chosen to sip the sweet wine of worldliness. The Church's stupor finds its roots in this very dilemma."[108]

---

[107] 2 Corinthians 10.4.

[108] Pastor Derek Melton.

Early Christian Persecution

Persecution started in the days of Israel's prophets. In Hebrews 11.33–38 we read:

> who by faith conquered kingdoms, administered justice, obtained promises, shut the mouths of lions, quenched the raging of fire, escaped the edge of the sword, gained strength after being weak, became mighty in battle, and put foreign armies to flight. Women received their dead—they were raised to life again. Some men were tortured, not accepting release, so that they might gain a better resurrection, and others experienced mockings and scourgings, as well as bonds and imprisonment. They were stoned, they were sawed in two, they died by the sword, they wandered about in sheepskins, in goatskins, destitute, afflicted, and mistreated. The world was not worthy of them. They wandered in deserts and on mountains, hiding in caves and holes in the ground.[109]

Persecution continued during the time of Christ and resulted in Him being crucified. After Jesus returned to heaven, Stephen was stoned to death. Persecution

---

[109] Jewish tradition says that it was Isaiah who suffered martyrdom by being sown in two under the orders of King Manasseh.

followed against all Christians in Jerusalem. The believers had to flee. Acts 8.4 says that those who were scattered went everywhere preaching the word. Scattered means they lost their homes, their jobs, their possessions, their families, and their friends. Yet they were empowered by the Holy Spirit and went everywhere preaching the word. They witnessed everywhere as persecution continued.

According to *Foxe's Book of Martyrs*,[110] here is how some early Church saints died according to the Bible, Church history, and tradition:

1. Stephen – Stoned
2. James, son of Zebedee – Beheaded
3. Philip – Crucified
4. Matthew – Slain
5. James, half-brother of Jesus – Stoned and head was smashed
6. Matthias – Stoned and beheaded
7. Andrew, Simon Peter's brother – Crucified
8. Mark – Dragged to death
9. Peter – Crucified upside down, he thought it not worthy to die in same manner of Jesus his Lord
10. Paul – Beheaded
11. Thaddeus – Crucified
12. Bartholomew – Crucified
13. Thomas – Speared
14. Luke – Hanged
15. Simon the Zealot – Crucified
16. John – Probably died in forced isolation

---

[110] John Foxe, *Foxe's Book of Martyrs* (Peabody: Hendrickson, 2004), chapter 1.

17. Barnabas - Martyred

We have all heard of the terrible persecutions in Rome and the Coliseum. Christians were thrown to the lions and other beasts. Nero had Christians tarred and burned, using them as lights in his garden. Please let what you just read sink in, let it sink in deep. Pray for it to penetrate.

Persecution throughout History

The book *Martyrs Mirror*[111] by Thieleman J. Van Braght, chronicles the unimaginable and horrible tortures of Christians throughout the ages. Hellish evil men with their demonically invented devices even exceeded those already mentioned. When reading the stories of the martyrs suffering for Christ, they spoke of and declared Christ Jesus to be sufficient in their trial, torture, and rejection.

Here is one such hero from the Middle Ages. A young man called Algerius. Not just young in years, but young in his faith. He was eventually killed in 1557. For those of us who are going through hard times, the response of young Algerius will help us.

Algerius wrote:

---

[111] Full title is *The Bloody Theater or Martyr's Mirror of the Defenseless Christians Who Baptized Only Upon Confession of Faith, and Who Suffered and Died for the Testimony of Jesus, Their Saviour, From the Time of Christ to the Year A. D. 1660* (Public domain).

In a dark hole I have found pleasure; in a place of bitterness and death, rest and hope of salvation; in the abyss or depths of hell, joy; where others weep, I have laughed; where others fear, I have found strength; who will believe this? In a state of misery I have had very great delight; in a lonely corner I have had most glorious company, and in the severest bond, great rest. All these things, my fellow brethren in Jesus Christ, the gracious hand of God has given me. Behold, He that at first was far from me, is now with me, and Him whom I knew but a little, I now see clearly; to whom I once looked from afar, Him I now behold as present; He for whom I longed, now offers me His hand; He comforts me; He fills me with joy; He drives from me bitterness, and renews within me strength and sweetness; He makes me well; He sustains me; He helps me up; He strengthens me. Oh, how good is the Lord, who does not suffer His servants to be tempted above that they are able.[112]

---

[112] http://www.biblerays.com/uploads/8/0/4/2/8042023/martyrs_mirror.pdf

Current Christian Persecution

On the internet it's easy to find pictures of Christians and their children martyred in the Middle East by beheading and many other atrocities. Stories of Christian persecution from many parts of the world such as North Korea, China, the Middle East, Africa, Asia, South America, and Mexico bring us to tears, move our hearts, and cause us to cry out to God.

Here's a story of great faith from Iran, where believers are widely persecuted. In Evin Prison, an infamous prison known for its torture, there's a group of Christians currently incarcerated. The prison Commander had them called and gave them a proposition, "If you promise to no longer share about salvation through Jesus Christ, we will release you." The Christians discussed it. The next day the Commander was told, "Sir, we appreciate your kind offer to release us but the salvation of God through His Son Jesus is so great we cannot make the promise you asked for." The Christians chose horrible prison conditions with torture and rape. They were not willing to stop speaking about the incredible Gospel of the Lord Jesus Christ. They're witnessing and sharing Christ in jail. Let us pray for them.

Christian persecution has started in North America at various levels. A Pastor in Canada, James Coates, has been jailed for holding Church meetings during the COVID-19 debacle.[113] The requirement of his release is that he must stop ministering, in other words, brother

---

[113] COVID-19 is definitely not what it seems. It's clearly not about health, it's about control.

Coates must stop obeying God. The evil hypocrisy is sickening because communities can have stores and other facilities open where hundreds of people gather, but Church meetings are absolutely forbidden.

Censorship and stripping away of Christian ministers' video channels and other social media platforms by YouTube, Facebook, Instagram, Twitter, Google, etc. is constantly happening and will get worse. The truth of the Gospel is being censored. The truth about what's happening is being silenced. This is not physical violence against the Body of Christ, but believers must be alert now because this is only the beginning stages of the flood of persecution that will come seemingly overnight.

Coming Christian Persecution

As the world changes at lightning speed. We are seeing a rapid progression toward a New World Order, a one world government, and a single world leader. The United Nations have a global plan called the 2030 Agenda to transform and enslave humanity with their vision of a utopian world. The United Nations and the Club of Rome, a secretive group of political and financial leaders, are planning 10 world regions. A one world religious system is evolving that will be led by a single religious leader, the Bible calls him the false prophet. This evil antichrist system will teach God is only love and the full acceptance of all faiths. Being an antichrist system it will also deny Jesus, the Son of the living God as the only way to God the Father. Thereby, Satan will attempt to send billions to an eternity in the Lake of Fire.

We are in the end times which is proven by an irrefutable sign, the return of Israel to its land that started in May 1948.[114] Other end times signs are: the spread of the Gospel and the growth of the Church worldwide (Matthew 16.18, 24.14), the increase of wickedness and the spread of evil (Matthew 24.12; 2 Timothy 3.1-5), the rise of false prophets and false/apostate religions (Matthew 24.4, 24; 2 Peter 2.1; 2 Corinthians 11.13; Jude 17-18), conflict or preparation for conflict in the Middle East (Matthew 24.6-7; Ezekiel 38.1-6), and the development of a global system which includes a global economy, government, and religion (Revelation 13.8-12, 16-17, 17.1-18).[115]

---

[114] Here are some verses that speak of the regathering of the people of Israel to the Holy Land: Isaiah 43.5-6; Ezekiel 20.34, and a two-stage gathering one physical and one spiritual in Ezekiel 37.1-14. Jews as a people have always existed since biblical times starting with Abraham, they have never ceased to exist. Jews have been dispersed throughout the world, and on May14, 1948, the state of Israel was established. This is known as the miracle of the modern state of Israel. No other ancient people group have survived global dispersion and oppression throughout their history, only Israel because they are God's original people that He will deal with during the Great Tribulation period that is soon approaching.

[115] Summarized from *The Harvest Handbook of Bible Prophecy*, 396-400. Helpful books that describe our current day and consider that we're near the end of the age are: Jimmy Evans, *Tipping Point: The End is Here* (Dallas: XO, 2020), and Terry James, ed., *Lawless: End-Times War against the Spirit of Antichrist* (Crane: Defender, 2020). Some video resources are: *The Coming Convergence* (2017), *The Daniel Project* (2012), and Don Stewart, *25 Signs We're near*

Christ Jesus spoke of the end times which will include international/national strife, famines, and natural disasters in many parts of the world. Jesus reminded us that all this is only the beginning of the birth pains with more to come. "They will hand you over for persecution and they will kill you. You will be hated by all nations because of My name" (Matthew 24.9). This will be worldwide.[116]

There are 195 countries in the world. Over 150 countries now have some form of opposition to Christianity, the one true God, and His Son Jesus Christ. The Christian faith has also deteriorated rapidly in the Western world. Speaking specifically about the nations of America and Canada, the end time signs that will soon lead to persecution are everywhere.

War has escalated against God and His commandments concerning purity, the family, morality, how God has biologically made men and women, and what we ultimately need to believe to have peace with God through His Son Jesus Christ. The Bible, prayer, and the Ten Commandments have been taken out of schools and most government offices. War has started against citizens which follow the "right." This includes the remnant true Church. As noted above there is also a war against free speech and truth by the censorship and propaganda of main stream media, including news outlets, television, and other tech platforms. There is war against conservative TV stations, war against conservative voices, and the LGBTQ sub-culture has great influence over politics, to

---

the End https://rumble.com/ve8ve3-hope-for-our-times-guest-speaker-don-stewart.html.

[116] Matthew 24-25; Mark 13; and Luke 21.

the point that the rainbow LGBTQ flag is currently raised at many U. S. embassies.

A radical Equality Act has been introduced into Congress that will affect churches, schools, hospitals, universities, businesses, day cares, and all government departments (basically all aspects of society). This proposal will likely pass with full support from the Biden administration. This includes allowing men to go into women's bathrooms and vice versa. Disney World is now honoring the LGBTQ agenda by presenting a transgender girl/boy for visiting children and parents to accept "alternate lifestyles." Amazon bans books that do not agree with Planned Parenthood. Godless leaders say that we must have a fully tolerant society, while hypocritically being intolerant of all conservative and/or biblical views.

A new Domestic Terrorism Prevention Act (DTPA) was proposed to Congress in January 2021. This act will deeply affect churches and Christians committed to God. A writer from the Ron Paul Institute summarizes the act as, *"The DTPA is essentially the criminalization of speech, expression, and thought. It takes cancel culture a step further and all but outlaws unpopular opinions. This act will empower intelligence, law enforcement, and even military wings of the American ruling class to crack down on individuals adhering to certain belief systems and ideologies."*[117]

There are FEMA (Federal Emergency Management Agency) retention camps and open graves all over the United States, yet empty. Some of these FEMA camps

---

[117] http://www.ronpaulinstitute.org/archives/featured-articles/2021/january/30/would-you-be-considered-a-domestic-terrorist-under-this-new-bill/ (Writer's emphasis).

may have guillotines. There's facial recognition software along with various levels of AI surveillance. Control of the masses is in progress via an unnecessary experimental gene-based injection. There are plans for vaccination passports. There are plans for mandatory universal vaccinations, and plans for the insertion of new tracking devices like digital chips or tattoos which are unified single-chip RFID type or quantum dot technological biomedical devices that store all our information.

The capabilities to control buying and selling are growing quickly while monetary systems will be switching to digital crypto-currencies replacing paper monies and coins.

The paragraphs above describe our current situation in much of North America (and the world). The stage is being set for Christian persecution and for others who are dissenters of the evil globalist agenda and who refuse to participate in this devilish system. Nazi Germany was a totalitarian system that led to devastating tyranny.

Dr. Gregory Stanton has documented *The Ten Stages of Genocide* which were used by Nazi Germany and which are apparent for North America today:

1. CLASSIFICATION: Distinguish people into "us and them." In Germany it was the Germans and the Jews. In America and Canada it is the "left" versus the "right."

2. SYMBOLIZATION: Symbols were used in Germany such as the yellow star and the swastika. Yellow stars had to be worn by the Jews. In

America it is now the COVID-19 mask; not wearing a mask is a symbol of defiance. Refusing the experimental gene-based "vaccine" will also be seen as defiant.

3. DISCRIMINATION: A dominant group denies freedom and the rights of others. This was done in Germany against all not of German Arian descent. Those in America on the right and following God will be denied freedoms by new legislation.

4. DEHUMANIZATION: Germany classified Jews not human. We now classify the unborn not human so that they can be killed. Likewise euthanasia laws are used to kill the elderly. In Canada a new bill is being introduced to euthanize the mentally handicapped. A holocaust followed in Germany. What will happen in America when those following God's laws are classified as not needed?

5. ORGANIZATION: Genocide is always organized, usually by the state. This was done in Germany killing Jews, other nationals, and the handicapped. The killing of children is organized by U. S. and Canadian governments. Contact tracing laws permit government representatives to enter any home they want and to take people into custody.[118]

---

[118] H. R. 6666 will likely be used to utilize mobile units to enter residences for COVID-19 testing and "other purposes." https://www.congress.gov/bill/116th-congress/house-bill/6666/text

6. POLARIZATION: Extremists drive the groups apart. Hate groups broadcast polarizing propaganda. Dissenting groups are silenced. This happened in Germany and is now happening in America by denying 1st Amendment rights and silencing conservatives. The "cancel culture" of trying to stop or strip away various levels of support from certain people and organizations because they have a certain point of view/belief is used against biblical morality and human reason.

7. PREPARATION: Plans were made for genocidal killings by Hitler. He planned the "Final Solution" for the Jewish. In the U. S. it will be thought of and called "counter-terrorism" under the Domestic Terrorism and Equality Acts. It will likely include COVID-19 and the final solution as proposed by Bill Gates and his plans for depopulating the world.[119]

---

[119] Bill Gates stated in a TED Talk, "First, we've got population. The world today has 6.8 billion people.

That's headed up to about nine billion. *Now, if we do a really great job on new vaccines, health care, reproductive health services, we could lower that by, perhaps, 10 or 15 percent.* But there, we see an increase of about 1.3." The context is a presentation on lowering CO_2 levels to zero. It's eerie how Gates' first factor in his equation is people, and Gates thinks that by lowering human population with "new vaccines," etc., this will help lower CO_2 levels. This man thinks he can play God and limit humanity's God-given mandate to multiply. Gates is a big proponent of Planned Parenthood. It's noteworthy that Gates' father was also involved with Planned Parenthood and eugenics. Bottom line, there are too many people on this planet and one of Gates' objectives is to lower the

8. PERSECUTION: Victims are identified and separated from society because of their ethnicity and/or religious identity, and will be separated because of beliefs and positions on certain issues. In Germany it was the Jews and others identified for concentration camps. In the U. S. and Canada, it will be quarantine facilities, health facilities, and likely FEMA camps. Some type of emergency will be declared using the World Health Organization (WHO) and/or the UN that will lead to genocide.

9. EXTERMINATION begins and quickly becomes the mass killing legally called "genocide." When this will start in North America we don't know. The killing of Christians in other countries of the world has been largely ignored by main stream media. In Revelation 20.4 we read of future beheadings of Christians on a global scale.

10. DENIAL is the final stage that follows genocide. Germans said, "We were just following orders." God says He will hold the guilty responsible. He says, "Vengeance is Mine, I will repay."[120]

---

population. Purely evil. https://www.ted.com/talks/bill_gates_innovating_to_zero/transcript#t-275601

[120] Summarized from Gregory H. Stanton's document, *The Ten Stages of Genocide*, https://www.scasd.org/cms/lib5/PA01000006/Centricity/Domain/1482/TenStages.pdf. Prophetically, Aldous Huxley and George Orwell both wrote about our current and soon coming dystopian New World Order in *Brave New World* and *1984* respectively. Some of *The Ten Stages of Genocide* can be seen

Don't Give Up

Therefore, since we have been declared righteous by faith, we have peace with God through our Lord Jesus Christ. We have also obtained access through Him by faith into this grace in which we stand, and we rejoice in the hope of the glory of God. And not only that, but we also *rejoice in our afflictions, because we know that affliction produces endurance, endurance produces proven character, and proven character produces hope* (Romans 5.1-4, writer's emphasis).

"[Believers] They conquered him [Satan] by the blood of the Lamb and by the word of their testimony, for they did not love their lives in the face of death" (Revelation 12.11). So we must participate. How? We overcome Satan, Antichrist, and overall evil by learning strategies given to us in the Bible. The Lord wants us, His people, to have an active part in overcoming evil and persecution. 1 Peter 4.12-19 tells us to *expect fiery trials*. What do we do then? Do we have a part? Do we sit back and do nothing? The following 20 key points will help prepare us for persecution. Choose some to work on. We do have a part:

1. Victory comes through Christ Jesus, His blood, the blood of the lamb. Without Him we can do nothing. This must be a daily acknowledgment. John 15.5; 1 Corinthians 15.57; Revelation 12.11.

---

in these works. In Deuteronomy 32.35 the Lord says this against evil doers, "Vengeance belongs to Me; I will repay. In time their foot will slip, for their day of disaster is near, and their doom is coming quickly."

2. We use the word of our testimony to overcome. We share how we were before we were saved, what happened when the Lord saved us, and we share how our life has changed and is being changed. 1 Peter 3.15; Revelation 12.11.

3. We love not our physical lives to the death. Embrace the Cross. Die to self-interest by placing God's priorities first. Romans 8.18, 12.1-2; Revelation 12.11.

4. We need to work on cultivating our relationship with and walking with Jesus. Romans 8.2; 1 Thessalonians 5.10; Matthew 28.20.

5. We need frequent filling by the Holy Spirit. Luke 11.13; Acts 1.8; Ephesians 5.18.

6. We need courageous faith, for faith is the victory. When Jesus returns will He see that we have faith? 1 John 5.4; Luke 18.8.

7. We need to be faithful in prayer and to pray without ceasing. Luke 18:1. Learn to pray as the persecuted did in Acts 4.24-31 and pray the prayer of the persecuted today:

   • Our persecution and suffering are our joy and honor.
   • We want to accept ridicule, scorn, and disadvantages with joy in Jesus' Name.

- We want to wipe others' tears away and comfort the suffering.
- We want to be ready to risk our lives because of our love for our neighbors, so that they also become Christians.
- We want to live our lives according to the standards set in God's Word.

8. We need to learn heavenly joy. The joy of the Lord is our strength. Learn to have joy. Luke 6.22-24, 10.20, 15.7; Psalm 16.11.

9. Love ardently and unconditionally even our enemies. Matthew 5.44. Start in your household. Forgive, love, bless, pray, and do good. 1 Corinthians 13.

10. Practice denying the flesh. Get along with less. Adjust your time for the Lord. Fast. Luke 9.23; Isaiah 58.6.

11. Memorize Scripture. Our Bibles may be taken away. Psalm 119.11.

12. Pray and seek out strong kindred spirit Christians whom you could fellowship with. It's a good idea to prepare with like-minded believers as persecution approaches.

13. Truly consider starting a house fellowship, especially if your church is closed or no longer teaching the Bible. Follow the pillars of a

biblical church in Acts 2.42. House churches were prominent in the early Church as seen in Acts 20.20; Romans 16.5; 1 Corinthians 16.19; Colossians 4.15; Philemon 2. It seems that persecution will lead back to house churches; the Church age is coming full circle.

14. Learn to be strong in the Lord as you put on the full armor of God. Ephesians 6.10-18.

15. Do a word search for martyr, persecute, persecution, witness, and hate in your Bible. Do you agree that God teaches us to be prepared for persecution and to give our lives? 1 Peter 4.12-19.

16. Read books, articles, and testimonies from the persecuted Church with your family. Familiarize yourself with *Foxe's Book of Martyrs* and ministries like Voice of the Martyrs, Open Doors, and others.

17. Learn to overcome fear. The antidote to fear is faith in the promises God gives us. They are eternal promises. Faith cancels out fear. Move from the house of fear to the house of faith. Luke 12.4-5 shows us not to fear those who can kill your body, but ultimately fear the Lord. Some of us are simply overwhelmed with fear. We worry about death through COVID-19. We worry about the "vaccine." We worry about inflation. We worry about job loss. We worry about income and finances. We worry about the future. Yet the Lord said He would never leave us nor forsake

us. God promised He would not press us beyond what we are able to bear. He wants us to use the antidote for fear He gave us. The antidote against fear is faith. *Faith is the ultimate victory!* Whatever has been born of God conquers the world. The victory that has conquered the world is the believer's FAITH! 1 John 5.4.

Corrie ten Boom and her family hid Jews during the Nazi era in Holland. Those who were found out would be sent to concentration camps to die. Corrie as a young girl was quietly weeping in her bed because of fear. Her father came and she shared with him her fears. She recalls:

> Father sat down on the edge of the narrow bed. "Corrie," he began gently, "when you and I go to Amsterdam by train, when do I give you your ticket?" I sniffed a few times, considering this. "Why, just before we get on the train." "Exactly. And our wise Father in heaven knows when we're going to need things, too. Don't run out ahead of Him, Corrie. When the time comes that some of us will have to die, you will look into your heart and find the strength you need, just in time."[121]

---

[121] Corrie ten Boom, *The Hiding Place* (Grand Rapids: Chosen, 1971).

Corrie's family was found out helping Jews. She was taken to a concentration camp where her sister died. Corrie lived and shared with the world *not to be afraid and to have faith in the Father's eternal promises.*

18. Where our lives fall short of a New Testament lifestyle we need to repent. 1 John 1.9.

19. We have to love our enemies and pray for our persecutors. When persecution comes we must do this, we'll need God's grace to. Matthew 5.44.

20. Are you willing to count the cost to truly follow Jesus even if it requires your life? Luke 14.25-33.

Truly pray and write your decision here: _____.

If you're a true born again Christian and you realize that your Christianity is not what it should be, perhaps you're not ready for persecution. Maybe your heart has grown a little cold, maybe it's hard toward the faith, or hard toward people, or you feel you can't really love others, or you feel you can't witness, or your commitment to Jesus is no longer what it once was, or you've lost the joy of your salvation, or you are not willing to accept persecution. Will you repent this day and ask the Lord for forgiveness, to cleanse, restore, and to help you?

Twenty points have been offered to you so you can be ready for persecution. Which points have brought a reminder to you from the Lord? Is there unbelief to repent from? Will you turn from it? What decision will you make? How will you go forward? Will you use any of the recommendations to work on to be ready?[122]

Summary

Stern persecution is coming. We've been informed and equipped so that we'll be ready for what's on the horizon, we *can* persevere through it, we *will* persevere through it. We are persecuted but not abandoned, the Lord's with us. Don't give up.

> *Those who are persecuted for righteousness are blessed, for the kingdom of heaven is theirs. You are blessed when they insult and persecute you and falsely say every kind of evil against you because of Me. Be glad and rejoice, because your reward is great in heaven. For that is how they persecuted the prophets who were before you.* – Jesus (Matthew 5.10-12)

---

[122] Here are some resources to help you be ready: Books – *Principles for the Gathering of Believers under the Headship of Jesus Christ*, https://christcenteredchristianity.com/resources/principles-book-gospel-fellowships/ and David Wilkerson, *God's Plan to Protect His People in the Coming Depression* (Lindale: Wilkerson Trust, 1998). Ministry of multiplying house churches – https://big.life/ .

HARDSHIPS,
DON'T GIVE UP

This is the second to last chapter, nonetheless in this section we're bringing home the previous chapters of not giving up. I believe *hardships* in one way or another best describe all the previous states we've examined: pain, pressure, perplexity, and persecution. In God's infinite wisdom expressed through His written word, He's given us two main keys so that we don't give up: His help and people's help. Let's briefly examine Scripture as we apply God's word to our lives aiming at victory.

Elements to Victory

The foundational text to this work is 2 Corinthians 4.8-9:

> *We are pressured in every way but not crushed; we are perplexed but not in despair; we are persecuted but not abandoned; we are struck down but not destroyed.*

As the apostle Paul and others were serving the Lord through serious life challenges, we see a contrasting pattern in the text, "we are _____ but not _____ ." The "we are" sections are best understood through a human struggle perspective, the "but not" sections are understood from the divine perspective of God's keeping grace of His people in these situations.

In essence we have, "*We're* pressured in life, but *by God's grace* we're not crushed." "*We're* perplexed in life, but *by God's grace* we're not hopeless." "*We're* persecuted in life, but *God's grace* sees us through as He's with us." "*We* experience hardships, but *by God's grace* we're not destroyed."[123]

Let me clarify, we have two main elements involved per event: the human and the divine. The keys to victory and not giving up are also dual: human and divine. Thus, God has shown us that through life's hardships one of His biblical designs for the believer's victory is to have two types of help working in unison: His help and other people's help. Yes and amen!

Divine Help

To successfully overcome life's hardships, we need the key element of God's help. Without God's help we'll struggle more than we have to, waste more time than we

---

[123] Let's remember that God's grace for the believer is God's supernatural power and kindness dispensed to us and ultimately has its origin in the person of Jesus. God's grace definitely includes His divine help to us in our time of need. See Ch.1. (Writer's emphasis).

should, and more often than not we'll end up frustrated. This is not God's will for His beloved children. God has promised us that we will neither be crushed, hopeless, abandoned, nor destroyed. I pray that you can see the biblical truth that when God is involved and we have His help in our hardships we can think of ourselves as being unstoppable and indestructible![124]

I believe that God is the Great Helper. By God being the most perfect being that can be conceived while having the attributes of omnipotence, omnipresence, and omniscience linked to His heart to help, no one is like Him. The Bible repeatedly shows and declares that God is humanity's supernatural helper:

- . . . God has the power to help . . . - *2 Chronicles 25.8*
- The LORD is my strength and my shield; my heart trusts in Him, and I am helped. – *Psalm 28.7*
- We wait for Yahweh; He is our help and shield. – *Psalm 33.20*
- God is our refuge and strength, a helper who is always found in times of trouble. – *Psalm 46.1*
- The LORD is my helper . . . - *Psalm 118.7*
- I lift my eyes toward the mountains. Where will my help come from? My help comes from the LORD, the Maker of heaven and earth. - *Psalm 121.1-2*
- I will strengthen you; I will help you . . . - *Isaiah 41.10*

---

[124] In the words of Billy Alsbrooks, we can be "blessed and unstoppable!"

- In truth, the LORD God will help me . . . - *Isaiah 50.9*
- To this very day, I have obtained help that comes from God . . . - *Acts 26.22*
- For since He [Jesus] Himself was tested and has suffered, He is able to help those who are tested. - *Hebrews 2.18*

A good example of divine help is found with a dear friend of mine, Jay from Liberia. Brother Jay, who was called to fulltime ministry by a deep sense to worship and serve the Lord, persevered by God's grace for ten years in completing his bachelor's degree in mathematics and economics from the University of Liberia. Throughout those ten years, Jay was literally running for his life during Liberia's brutal tribal civil wars (1989-2003).

Running from vicious warlords like General Butt Naked took its toll,[125] but Jay was focused not to give up as the Lord had him involved in reaching the lost through campus ministry. To this day, Brother Jay has constantly relied upon God's help to plant dozens of house churches throughout West Africa in the countries of Liberia, Sierra Leon, and Guinea. Jay continues welcoming God's help as he perseveres in serving the Lord through the frequent

---

[125] General Butt Naked was the warlord name for Joshua Milton Blahyi who mercilessly and barbarically killed thousands during Liberia's tribal wars. BUT GOD had mercy on Joshua and miraculously saved his soul, Joshua has deeply repented and has been serving the Lord as a powerful evangelist since his conversion to Christ. I asked Brother Jay about Joshua's conversion, Jay said it's truly genuine. Hallelujah!

hardships of typhoid fever and malaria. In his words, "We can't give up on what God has called us to do."

People's Help

Another key element needed to successfully overcome life's hardships is people's help. Created as social creatures we were never meant to bear life and its burdens alone. Surely there are times when we should be alone to think, meditate, work, study, be with God, etc. However, much of life normally consist of interdependent relationships between people. We need others to help us as we help those who need our help. Together we can reach victory in and through our hardships. When we help one another, God is glorified while thanksgiving to Him multiplies.

Great Britain's Derek Redmond, at the 1992 Barcelona Olympic games, was in full stride in the 400-meter semi-final race when he pulled his hamstring and fell. While he hobbled in agony to finish, Derek's father stormed the track and helped his son across the finish line in what became one of the most touching and inspiring displays of loving help in history.

Another example of the human help element is when two athletes helped each other at the 2016 Rio Olympic games. In what some call the most beautiful moment of the Olympics, American runner Abbey D'Agostino (Cooper), and New Zealand's Nikki Hamblin, both fell during a 5000-meter contest. Immediately after the collision, Abbey helped Nikki to her feet and encouraged her to keep going. Nikki also helped Abbey, who suffered several injuries, complete the race in severe pain.

In Abbey's words, "Although my actions were instinctual at that moment, the only way I can and have rationalized it is that God prepared my heart to respond that way . . . this whole time here He's made clear to me that my experience in Rio was going to be about more than my race performance -- and as soon as Nikki got up, I knew that was it."[126]

As I reflect on these two public displays of people helping people to continue and succeed, I can't help but to think that perhaps these two examples are what God intended for humanity to see on a world stage. Yes, these examples are from sports, but the applications could be limitless. In these episodes we witness people's love, care, encouragement, grit, selflessness, courage, beauty, strength, determination, endurance, pain, and we see all these things being intermingled with deep heartfelt tears. Profoundly beautiful.[127]

As Christians, we must help one another as others help us. We can't do it alone. If we try to succeed alone, when times get tough we won't persevere too well. Sometimes God uses us, you and me, to be the answer to someone's cry for help, and vice versa sometimes when others help us is how God answers our prayers for help.

---

[126] https://abcnews.go.com/Sports/abbey-dagostino-helped-competitor-fall-final-torn-acl/story?id=41456464

[127] Both Derek Redmond's and Abbey D'Agostino and Nikki Hamblin's deeply encouraging events can be found on the internet. Please watch them both and take a few minutes in reflection.

Don't Give Up

The key in persevering through life's hardships is to have God's help while allowing others in our lives to aid us unto victory. Our Lord is a God who values communication. He also values when we communicate with each other voice to voice and especially face to face.

In our digital age, there's nothing wrong with texting, but we mustn't lose the human aspect of a well-timed uplifting phone call or a beautiful time of face to face encouraging fellowship. As our current society mistakenly thinks that two or more people being around each other without a face mask is a health crisis, this is nothing but the enemy that wants us to stay alone, stay discouraged, and ultimately be defeated.

The Bible is clear that God wants us to meet face to face for encouragement and edification. The apostle John in two of his epistles wrote (almost verbatim), "I hope to be with you and talk face to face so that our joy may be complete." "I hope to see you soon, and we will talk face to face."[128] The reason God emphasizes us to meet in person whenever we can is because when two or more are gathered in the Name of Jesus He is in the midst while His Spirit lifts our countenance.[129] God takes great pleasure in being among His people as we encourage and help one another. Our own spirits are lifted as we help another saint persevere in hardship. By doing this, in God's eyes our joy may be complete!

---

[128] 2 John 12; 3 John 14 respectively.
[129] Matthew 18.20.

Perhaps in this season you're feeling lonely and desire deeper relationships. Then please ask the Lord to help you find true Christian friendships. Ask the Lord to surround you with kindred spirits in which the Holy Spirit helps everyone grow in grace and in the knowledge of the Lord Jesus. I believe that the Lord will delight to answer your prayers through the Church or through another blessed avenue.

Here are some verses and examples that show God's grace working through people as they were there for one another:

- . . . there's a friend who stays closer than a brother. — *Proverbs 18.24*
- Two are better than one because they have a good reward for their efforts. For if either falls, his companion can lift him up; but pity the one who falls without another to lift him. — *Ecclesiastes 4.9-10*
- Ruth and Naomi — *Ruth 1.16-17*
- David and Jonathan — *1 Samuel 18.1, 20.17, 20.41-42; 2 Samuel 1.26*
- Jesus' dear friends of Mary, Martha, and Lazarus — *John 11*
- Some of Paul's friends — *Romans 16.3-16*

Summary

When we have both God's and other people's help being poured into us during our moments of hardship, there is no reason that we should ever quit. God's grace is extended to us through people, which in turn causes thanksgiving to increase to God's glory.[130] As mentioned, life's pains, pressures, perplexities, and persecutions are all under the umbrella of hardships. The best way to thrive (not just survive) through hardships, whether small or large, is to have God ordained help, divine and human. It's time to persevere!

---

[130] 2 Corinthians 4.15.

A TIME TO GIVE UP

This book's main focus has been tied to encouraging us not to give up and to persevere through life's challenges. In this last chapter, I want to present the truth that there are times when we should give up. In these times of giving up, I'm convinced that God is honored and that it's the best decision to make.

Rhythms of Life

In the genre of wisdom literature found in the Bible, we encounter the book of Ecclesiastes, the book of the Preacher/Teacher who contemplates life under the sun (life on earth). Many Bible scholars believe that the Preacher/Teacher is King David's son, Solomon, the wisest person who ever lived. Led by the Spirit of God, some of his wisdom is shared with us in the book's most famous passage, a highly structured poem which considers that throughout the normal rhythms of life there's a time for everything:

> *There is a time for everything, and a season for*
> *every activity under heaven:*
> *a time to be born and a time to die,*
> *a time to plant and a time to uproot,*
> *a time to kill and a time to heal,*
> *a time to tear down and a time to build,*
> *a time to weep and a time to laugh,*
> *a time to mourn and a time to dance,*
> *a time to scatter stones and a time to gather*
> *them,*
> *a time to embrace and a time to refrain,*
> *a time to search and A TIME TO GIVE UP,*
> *a time to keep and a time to throw away,*
> *a time to tear and a time to mend,*
> *a time to be silent and a time to speak,*
> *a time to love and a time to hate,*
> *a time for war and a time for peace.*[131]

These heavenly words open with the idea that there's a time for every occurrence and a season in which that occurrence happens, "*There is a time for everything, and a season for every activity under heaven.*" This statement is both descriptive and prescriptive of the fourteen sets of opposites that follow. Descriptive in the sense that the words illustrate what is plain to humanity, normal events like these take place at certain times in life. The words are also prescriptive, they direct the reader/listener to take proper action at the proper time. For example, "there's a time to weep and a time to laugh" is understood two ways, that these actions occur in life, and that they are also

---

[131] Ecclesiastes 3.1-8 (NIV, writer's emphasis).

the proper actions to take at the right time (e.g., weeping at a funeral, laughing at a comedy).

Given the fourteen sets of opposites (3.2-8) that we broadly experience, the center point of this chapter will be the truth presented as "a time to give up."

Time to Give Up

In the chapter on pain, I mentioned that I was at the Mayo Clinic. I was there with my wife, Jennifer, who was being treated for her complex health issues. After battling sicknesses that violently stripped her health away for over a decade, someone recommended that the Mayo Clinic may be beneficial.

Throughout Jennifer's health afflictions, we've ran the gamut of doctors, procedures, medicines, supplements (artificial and natural), prayer, confession of sin, anointing with oil, fasting, faith intercessors, healing ministries, etc. At times, these things brought hope and encouragement, but she continued to get sick.

As her husband, I stayed in prayer, trusted the Lord, supported, comforted, and guided her the best that I could. However, the years of seeing Jennifer waste away beat me down. I started to get stressed and depressed, even though I could still function at a fairly high level, I was truly living life by running on fumes of hope, and I knew it. Something had to change, that something was someone, me. I had to learn the art of giving up. So, the Lord taught me.

Before visiting the Mayo Clinic, there was a failed attempt with a critical procedure by a renowned specialist in Jennifer's area of disease in which I hit a life wall, hard. Soon after this disappointing occasion, I had several days of solitude. Just me and God. No phone, no computer, no food. Just the Bible, some resources, and silence in which to pray and to hear from God.

After a couple days of weeping and pouring out my heart to the Lord, the Spirit of God tenderly and powerfully spoke to me. He spoke to my spirit as I read *Walking through Twilight* by Douglas Groothuis, Groothuis' raw and stirring account of dealing with his own wife's illness. In the book, there's a short chapter "Giving Up," that the Lord used mightily to get my attention. The Lord was working on me with His jackhammer of love.

I told the Lord that I wasn't ready to obey what He was impressing on my heart to do. After about 36 hours, I succumbed – I truly, like never before, gave it all to Him. I gave up. I gave up the burden that was too heavy for me to carry. I gave up the stress that was crushing me and taking some of my joy. I gave both these items and more to the Lord as I confessed my sin of stubbornly not giving up, and not giving all of life's issues to Him.

In my giving up, I felt a tremendous pressure lifted from my soul. The pressures and stresses have never returned, they won't. These items that I carried for years will never come back because they have been fully placed in the Lord's hands.[132] As I write, Jennifer is slowly being restored from her affliction with the spirit of infirmity,

---

[132] 1 Peter 5.7 comes to mind, "casting all your care on Him, because He cares about you." Jesus said in Matthew 11.28, "Come to Me, all you who are weary and burdened, and I will give you rest."

we believe that she'll be fully restored in God's perfect time. I'm at total peace with this, there's been a true liberating change in my heart since I gave up. The words of the Lord are true, there's a time to give up.

There's a time to give up, and there's also a way to give up. The Preacher/Teacher continues, ". . . a wise heart knows the right time and procedure. For every activity there is a right time and procedure, even though man's troubles are heavy on him" (8.5-6). When we give up, we must approach the Lord in a certain way and give up in a certain way, I believe that way is with a humble heart and lowly spirit of dependence. Let us recognize that He cares for us like no other can. Let us realize that He can truly deal with our hardest and saddest life issues in a way that brings us His true peace that passes all understanding. The method of giving up is a wise way, a tender way, a humbling way, a healing way, and a heavenly way.

Yes, there's great satisfaction in not giving in, pushing through, and reaching goals. There's also tremendous beauty in not giving up as we meet life's challenges. Nonetheless, when we wisely give up properly and at the right time elegance is also discovered. As God works in our hearts, we will know when the time of futile persevering is at hand. Some life issues/problems are not for us to take on with stubborn arrogant sinful perseverance. I believe that you and I will know when we *should* keep fighting and persevering, I also believe that we'll also know when God is making it clear that we *should* give up.

One major way to know when to give up is to have the peace of God in the decision. God is spirit and by His Spirit He communicates to our spirit. God lovingly directs (and when needed corrects) our steps. Some lessons may take us weeks, months, and even years to learn. Let's remember that God is not like us, He's patient with us as He molds us to the perfect image of Jesus His Son. With that said, when we decide to throw in the towel and give in, the Lord will grant us a deep peace to confirm that the decision to give up is right.

People around us may not understand our decision to give in. But, that's between us and the Lord. In our hearts we will know that it's the right decision at the right time. It's a personal relationship with the Lord that we have, He speaks to each of us differently, and has our best interest always at heart. He will never misguide us.

Is It Time to Give Up?

What is it in your life that the Lord has been speaking to you about to give up and to give wholly to Him? Is there something that has been burdening you for a long time? Do you need release from the pressures and stresses of not giving up when you should? Have you been working against God's grain, not working with Him but against Him? Do you need clarity of if and when you should give up? Should you spend time shut in with God, seeking His face, and pouring out your heart so that you can finally give up as you give it all to Him? Is now the time for you to give up and place all your burdens and cares in His loving hands?

I hope that our Lord has been speaking to your heart. As I learned how to honestly give my deepest cares and concerns to Him, I know that you will also be blessed in the grace of giving up when it's your time to do so. There is a proper time to give up, may the Lord guide you in when and how to do it. He's patiently waiting.

Summary

There's a time for everything. When it's time to give up, give up. He will let you know.

A WATCHMAN'S UNSCIENTIFIC MEDITATION OF REASONABLE RANDOM THOUGHTS

I understand enough to know that all of us have been on a stretching journey since the COVID mess began. It's been difficult. Heart breaking. Thought provoking. Suspicion raising. But it's also been encouraging. Encouraging to experience the veracity of God's word. Encouraging to know that the Lord has laid many thoughts on my mind, impressed some on my heart, and has allowed me to formulate some. What follows are what I think could be some of the thoughts that some of us have but can't quite express, if you are one of those or one of us, then I humbly ask you to allow me to be your mouth-piece.

If we haven't noticed, the world has been shaken and is still shaking, at the very least God is allowing this or perhaps He's doing it directly. I am quite certain that based on the character of God, a Being who commands repentance from His creatures who've been made in His image, the world is being called to wake up, smell the iniquity, and to repent from it. And/or from another view, we could put it this way, the deaf church is being blared toward megaphone style to awaken from its slumber and to smell the napalm of the spiritual war. Since earth dwellers have no interests in the purposes of God, the last statement stands.

"WIDESPREAD DECEPTION, WORLD'S HURTING, JESUS' RETURN SOON" so says my bumper magnet. Deception at a grand scale is taking place, tremendous amounts of lies. Global lies. National lies. Local lies. Government lies. Media lies. Most people don't have ears to hear these lies, and they don't have the eyes to see the lies.

Satan is the lying deceiver and the god of this lying age. He is consciously and unconsciously the lord of many people; he is the lord of the *flies*. This meditation is not about Beelzebub, it's about what he and his cohorts represent, mainly: sin, death, and destructive deception all through lies. Deception is cunning craftiness, cleverness to lead astray even the elect. What started in the Garden has multiplied exponentially. One main form of *the lie* that the world is experiencing is propaganda.

Propaganda, not the poet from Cali, is the information designed to persuade people to accept an idea/concept and to join some type of cause. Propaganda uses biased material and greatly rides on people's emotions, their feelings. Propaganda is manipulation. Here's an excerpt from a famous work's chapter on propaganda and its use to control the masses:

> The receptive powers of the masses are very restricted, and *their understanding is feeble.* On the other hand, *they quickly forget.* Such being the case, *all effective propaganda* must be confined to *a few bare essentials* and *those must be expressed as far as possible in stereotyped formulas. These slogans should be persistently repeated until the very last individual has come to grasp the idea that has been put forward.*[133]

Please read the excerpt a few times and let it sink in. In essence, what the text means is that people are stupid and they forget everything, so propaganda in forms of slogans that are aimed toward a person's feelings will be greatly effective in ultimately having them buy into the idea and cause. This text is from *Mein Kampf* by Adolph Hitler. Please linger on that. Let us not forget what Hitler's demonic lies led to.

COVID-19 is the only virus/sickness in history that has had its own PR propaganda campaign. Globally, from the avenues of media, retail shops, to fortune five hundred corporations we are being assaulted 24/7 with slogans such as: "We're all in this together" "Mask up" "Do your part" "Stop the spread" etc., all for a coronavirus that has a 99.8% recovery rate that is being used to strip away individual's basic rights, freedoms, and in some cases strip away psychological stability.

---

[133] Adolf Hitler, chapter six "War Propaganda" in *Mein Kampf* (Public domain). (Writer's emphasis).

If we weren't firmly told daily that we're in a pandemic, then no one would even have a clue that there was one, even if it was planned. Lying propaganda has been and is being used to systematically deconstruct and reconstruct the world with an agenda to fully control and monitor the people in it.

Coronaviruses are real, the vast majority of people dying from COVID due to comorbidities is also a reality. Manufactured plandemics are also genuine. Authentic propagated COVID expressions are being used to manipulate people and get everybody on the same page, and when anybody dissents from the popular narrative and its narrators, they are either censored, ignored, attacked, or maligned (in most cases a mix or all of these are experienced). However, some of us do critically observe what's going on, we do think, we do read, and we do believe the Bible, so we know where these events are headed. Let's remember these words, *"You can fool all the people some of the time, and some of the people all the time, but you cannot fool all the people all the time."*[134]

Let's step back for a minute and witness the deep division that COVID propaganda has created. The experimental gene therapy injection "vaccine" that is being mandated for all of humanity has immediately created a divide. People who decide not to get the unnecessary exploratory operating system inoculation, which doesn't stop transmission and afterwards you still have to "mask up" and "social distance," are being seen as part of the problem.

This gene therapy is causing a two-tier society. We

---

[134] Attributed to Abraham Lincoln. (Writer's emphasis).

have the vaxxed on one side and the non-vaxxed on the other, and the mentality is growing that the non-vaxxed shouldn't be able to participate in this brave new world. Is this an early picture of the division of people who will willingly receive the mark of the beast and people who don't receive the mark as they refuse to worship the beast? (The COVID gene therapy is not the mark of the beast because the beast has yet to be revealed).

Back to our reasoned random thought, this deception, all out psychological warfare to socially condition the undiscerning masses, is led by global elites and technocrats. These godless people are unelected officials that are running the world. Sadly, the majority of the world's population are uncritically obeying the edicts they're given. We're seeing the final pieces put in place before the full-blown Bible predicted one-world government, one-world economic system, and the one-world religion led by the final Antichrist and the false Prophet are fully functional. I believe we're only seconds away.

Jesus told us to watch out so that we're not deceived (Matthew 24). Discerners of the times can relate to the following, *"They lie to us, we know they're lying, they know we know they're lying, but they keep lying to us."*[135]

Aside from outer propaganda, there's another form of falsehood, *inner self-deception*, call it willful ignorance. People by their own volition choose to not look at data/ evidence, because it goes against their held beliefs and/or what they've been (wrongly) told or commanded to do.

For example, there are multitudes of individuals and groups who have been diligently working to share

---

[135] Attributed to Alexander Solzhenitsyn. (Writer's emphasis).

true data of this plandemic, which when these truths are accepted can work toward hope as it dispels the prevalent spirit of fear. Still, when truthful articles and/or videos are shared with people, the vast majority of people simply refuse to even look/listen to the data that could save their lives. I've never seen this in my life, people who care about others are lovingly and truthfully telling them that they're headed toward a cliff, and people still choose to keep going toward the cliff full speed ahead no matter what! This is pure insanity!

After humanity's general rejection of God and His truths, are we seeing or is this a foreshadowing of some type of 2 Thessalonians 2 God sent delusion? Perhaps we're witnessing Romans 1 where God gives people over to darkened senseless minds from which they can't reason. Or maybe the popular idiom "it's easier to believe a lie than the truth" is a convenient reality, as it's much easier to apathetically not think and be a Lemming or be one of the Sheeple who's headed toward a brutal totalitarian communism which has its roots connected with the Lake of Fire. All in all, the following words are descriptively accurate of the masses' mindstate: "It is easier to believe a lie that one has heard a thousand times than to believe a fact [truth] that one has never heard before."[136]

Undoubtedly, willful ignorance is one thing that leads a person straight to hell. In John 5, the Lord Jesus tells the religious establishment that there are multiple witnesses pointing to the truth of who He is; God the Father, John the Baptist, Jesus' sign miracles, and the OT Scriptures all testify that Jesus is the Messiah. But the powers that

---

[136] Attributed to Robert Lynd.

be and many others willfully refuse to believe the data of who Jesus is. Jesus plainly says, *"you are not willing to come to Me so that you may have life"* (John 5.40, emphasis added). Jesus also lamented over Jerusalem when many willfully rejected him (Matthew 23.37).

A person's volition keeps them from salvation, a person's free will keeps them from knowing the truth and being set free. This is indeed some of what we're seeing happen in the world. People simply *refuse to look at and trust evidence that will help them*, both types natural and spiritual data are being willfully ignored.

Not only is the Gospel and evidence that we've been globally lied to being willfully ignored, but headlines are being willfully ignored. Headlines like *"Former Pfizer VP And Chief Scientist – [Says] 'Entirely Possible This [Vaccine] Will Be Used For Massive-scale Depopulation'"* *"'The Great Reset' Is Just An Updated Blueprint For The New World Order"* *"80,000 More Retail Stores To Close As COVID Shifts Spending To Online"* *"Massive U.S. Food Shortage Coming"* Our willful ignorance of these warnings of looming destruction is not cute nor humorous, it is categorical foolishness.

I'm saddened and sure that willful ignorance will not be reversed anytime soon, because at the time of the end the wicked will keep doing wickedly, but the wise will understand (Daniel 12.10). In other words, God seekers (the true truth seekers), will have an idea of what's truly going on around them (as they have been informed by God's prophetic Scriptures), but the unbelieving world will keep thinking and acting like the unbelieving world.

In this late hour of the last stage of the Church age,

we believers need to do two things: keep our eyes fixed upon Jesus and keep looking to the Lord for spiritual strength, His armor, and wisdom. Keeping our eyes fixed on Jesus (Hebrews 12.2) means to keep trusting Jesus. In Jesus' conversation with Nicodemus (John 3), Jesus tells Nicodemus that like the bronze serpent that was raised in the wilderness (Numbers 21), He, Jesus, will also be lifted up and grant salvation to all who would look (trust) to Him. We have to keep trusting in Jesus and He will keep us close to Him as He protects us from the plans of the enemy.

We also need God-given spiritual strength, the full armor of God, and wisdom like never before. Before the apostle Paul presented the armor of God in Ephesians 6, he stated that we must be strong in the Lord and in God's power; this spiritual strength comes from God who is Spirit. By faith we need to be equipped with the full armor of God. Wisdom comes from the all-wise God. The Lord will equip us in this dark season, to stand for truth, stand for others, all while we stand boldly for Christ.

We can fully and confidently trust Jesus and look to the Lord to supply what we need. There is no telling how much global destruction and pressure the saints will endure before Jesus' return.

Staying informed is a deep necessity right now, people perish for lack of knowledge, let's not be part of the perishing. Stay informed with trustworthy updates and newsletters by Tom Hughes *Hope for Our Times*, JD Farag *Prophecy Update,* and *Prophecy News Watch*. From a medical and health perspective *America's Frontline Doctors* and *Children's Health Defense* are informative and helpful. I can't urge you enough to share the truth that you're being equipped with. Find a group of like-minded believers to fellowship with as you faithfully evangelize and make disciples waiting on the return of the Lord.

We must be watching and praying. When Jesus returns will He find faith on the earth or will we be considered the most inattentive, sleepy, undiscerning church generation ever to exist?[137] God has us perfectly placed in this time in history to be His witnesses (martyrs). He'll send Jesus in His own perfect time. I urge you to give your all to the Lord and to trust Him and His purposes. In eternity, it'll be of eternal worth. Those who have ears let them hear. Don't give up. *Maranatha!*

---

[137] Paraphrased from Jeff Kinley, *Aftershocks: Christians Entering a New Era of Global Crisis* (Eugene: Harvest House, 2021), 9.

A MESSAGE OF TRUE HOPE: THE GOSPEL OF JESUS CHRIST

We were created in the image of the LORD God of the Bible, the only true God. He is holy, righteous, just, loving, gracious, and compassionate. We all have sinned against Him. Sin causes separation from God. The wages of sin is death with an ultimate destiny in eternal hell. This is indeed bad news. But there is indeed good news, the Gospel. God demonstrated His love for the world by coming to earth in His One and Only Son – Jesus the Messiah who was born in Israel. Jesus fulfilled God's laws and lived a perfect life. Jesus paid the full penalty of God's wrath against sin when He died on a cross as a substitute on behalf of all the people who would ever believe in Him. He was buried, then He physically resurrected from the dead; this proved that God accepted Jesus' substitutionary atoning death so that people can be forgiven their sins and be reconciled to God.

God commands every person to turn from their sins and to receive Jesus by faith. The person who does this will be spiritually born again and receive eternal life along with a new relationship in which they can now call God, Father, and fully participate in His Kingdom when Jesus returns as King.

> This is the message of faith that we proclaim: If you confess with your mouth, "Jesus is Lord," and believe in your heart that God raised Him from the dead, you will be saved. One believes with the heart, resulting in righteousness, and one confesses with the mouth, resulting in salvation. Now the Scripture says, Everyone who believes on Him will not be put to shame, for there is no distinction between Jew and Greek, since the same Lord of all is rich to all who call on Him. For everyone who calls on the name of the Lord will be saved. – *Romans 10.8-13*

I urge you to make the destiny-changing decision to believe the Gospel of Jesus Christ and to receive Jesus through prayer as you call on Him to be the Lord of your life and Savior of your soul.★ Things are going to get worse. God is showing us that there is no other true hope in this world other than turning from our sin and trusting in Him through Jesus Christ.

Our times are uncertain and unsteady,
it's too hard to stand, it's time for us to
kneel.

I pray that you have ears to hear. He's
coming soon.

*One way to know if your salvation is true is to read 1 John and measure your life by it. The Lord will help you live a life that pleases Him so you can be ready for Jesus' return.

HELPFUL RESOURCES

ENCOURAGING BIBLE VERSES

Perseverance must finish its work so that you may be mature and complete, not lacking anything.

James 1.4-5 (NIV)

Let us not become weary in doing good, for at the proper time we will reap a harvest if we do not give up.

Galatians 6.9 (NIV)

Blessed is the man who perseveres under trial, because when he has stood the test, he will receive the crown of life that God has promised to those who love Him.

James 1.12 (NIV)

Therefore we do not give up. Even though our outer person is being destroyed, our inner person is being renewed day by day.

2 Corinthians 4.16 (NIV)

Then Jesus told his disciples a parable to show them that
they should always pray and not give up.
Luke 18.1 (NIV)

I love You, LORD, my strength.
Psalm 18.1 (HCSB)

I am able to do all things
through Him who strengthens me.
Philippians 4.13 (HCSB)

My flesh and my heart may fail,
but God is the strength of my heart
and my portion forever.
Psalm 73.26 (NIV)

Those who know your name will trust in you, for you,
LORD, have never forsaken those who seek you.
Psalm 9.10 (NIV)

The LORD is good to those whose hope is in him, to the
one who seeks him.
Lamentations 3.25 (NIV)

Without faith it is impossible to please God, because
anyone who comes to him must believe that he exists
and that he rewards those who earnestly seek him.
Hebrews 11.6 (NIV)

But seek first the kingdom of God and
His righteousness, and all these things will be
provided for you. Therefore, don't worry about

tomorrow, because tomorrow will worry about itself.
Each day has enough trouble of its own.

Matthew 6.33-34 (HCSB)

RECOMMENDED READING

Aftershocks: Christians Entering a New Era of Global Crisis,
    Jeff Kinley

Bible Promises for You (NIV), Zondervan

Believer's Bible Commentary, William MacDonald

Corona False Alarm?: Facts and Figures, Sucharit Bhakdi and
    Karina Reiss

COVID Operation, Pam A. Popper and Shane D. Prier

God's Plan to Protect His People in the Coming Depression,
    David Wilkerson

The Harvest Handbook of Bible Prophecy, eds. Ed Hindson,
    Mark Hitchcock, and Tim LaHaye

Have You Felt Like Giving Up Lately?, David Wilkerson

Lawless: End Times War against the Spirit of Antichrist, ed.
    Terry James

The Moody Bible Commentary, eds. Michael Rydelnik and
    Michael Vanlaningham

Pandemics, Plagues, and Natural Disasters, Erwin Lutzer

*The Price of Panic: How the Tyranny of Experts Turned a
    Pandemic into a Catastrophe*, Douglas Axe, William M.
    Briggs, and Jay W. Richards

*Principles for the Gathering of Believers under the Headship of
    Jesus Christ*, Gospel Fellowships

Tipping Point: The End is Here, Jimmy Evans

Walking through Twilight, Douglas Groothuis

INFORMATIVE WEBSITES

www.jdfarag.org – JD Farag – *Prophecy Updates*

www.hopeforourtimes.com – Tom Hughes – *Prophecy Updates and News (Christian worldview)*

www.olivetreeviews.org – Jan Markell – *Prophecy Updates and News (Christian worldview)*

www.hischannel.com/BreakingNewsMonday – *Live/ Video News (Christian worldview)*

www.prophecynewswatch.com – *News (Christian prophetic worldview)*

www.zerohedge.com – *News (non-Christian worldview)*

www.americasfrontlinedoctors.org – *Group of doctors and medical professionals - USA*

www.worlddoctorsalliance.com – *Group of doctors and medical professionals - Worldwide*

www.childrenshealthdefense.org – *Informative news on vaccines and health (Robert Kennedy Jr.)*

DOCUMENTARIES/FILMS

www.thecomingconvergence.com – *Prophetic documentary film*

www.studioscotland.com/thedanielproject – *Prophetic documentary film*

www.planetlockdownfilm.com – *Informative documentary film and interviews*

https://seeing2020.uscreen.io/ - *Seeing 2020: The Censored Science of The COVID-19 Pandemic*

BASIC HEALTH TIPS

- Start each day with 30 minutes of prayer and Bible reading, present yourself to God as a living sacrifice, ask the Lord Jesus to help you deny yourself and to help you die daily to your own self interests as you prioritize the Lord's purposes
- Drink mostly water and stay hydrated
- Try to eat at least 80% clean/healthy
- If over 30 years old consider high quality digestive enzymes and HCL
- Exercise 5-6 times per week. Perhaps start with 2 to 3, 20–30-minute walks. Running and CrossFit type HIIT exercises are beneficial. (During exercise don't wear a mask; you'll hyperventilate, may faint, or something worse could happen)
- Boost your immune system with high quality vitamin C, vitamin D, and zinc supplements
- Find healthy ways to relieve stress
- Find healthy ways to relax